Fancy Fruits
AND
Extraordinary
Vegetables

A Guide to Selecting,
Storing, & Preparing

ℱANCY
FRUITS
AND
ℰXTRAORDINARY
VEGETABLES

BY SANDRA C. STRAUSS

Illustrated by Mac Access

HASTINGS HOUSE · BOOK PUBLISHERS
Mamaroneck, N.Y.

To Rick, Stephanie, and Stacy
With love and appreciation

ISBN 0-8038-9335-3
Library of Congress Catalog Card Number 91–074151

Printed in the United States of America

Distributed by Publishers Group West, Emeryville, California

CONTENTS

$\mathcal{P}$HOTO CREDITS

Cover photography by Mark Huelsbeck, courtesy of J. R. Brooks & Son.

Photographs of the following courtesy of United Fresh Fruit & Vegetable Association: kumquat; Hachiya persimmons; Fuyu persimmons; plantains; mango; gingerroot; prickly pear; spaghetti squash; kohlrabi; chili peppers; cilantro/jícama/chayote/tomatillos; chayote; fennel; alfalfa sprouts/bean sprouts; specialty array; pomegranate; chinese cabbage/celery cabbage; quince; rhubarb; bok choy; Jerusalem artichokes.

Photographs of the following courtesy of J. R. Brooks & Son: atemoya; carambola; chayote; mamey; lychees; passion fruit.

Photographs of the following courtesy of California Tropics: cherimoya; feijoa; passion fruit; white sapote.

Photograph of kiwi courtesy of California Kiwifruit Commission.

Photograph of Asian pears courtesy of Phillips Farms & Universal Produce Corporation.

Photograph of sugar snap peas courtesy of Rogers NK Seed Company.

Photograph of arugula courtesy of The Green House Fine Herbs.

Photograph of artichoke courtesy of California Artichoke Advisory Board.

Photograph of papaya courtesy of Papaya Administrative Committee.

$\mathcal{A}$CKNOWLEDGMENTS

A book is a combination of many talents, and I am grateful for all those who provided assistance, support, encouragement, knowledge, and inspiration.

The fresh produce industry is filled with generous hearts and wise souls. Many thanks to Peter Nichols at California Tropics; Stephanie Johnson and Bill Schaefer at J. R. Brooks & Son, Inc., and Amy Chang and Chris Martin at New Zealand Gourmet for providing many of the tropical delights featured in this book as well as a wealth of information.

I also want to express appreciation for all those produce pros who provided photos, information, and guidance: Patty Boman, California Artichoke Advisory Board; Becker Communications on behalf of the Papaya Administrative Committee; Tom Anderson, Calavo Growers of California; the helpful information team at Frieda's Finest of California; Donna Greenbush, The Green House; California Kiwifruit Commission; Elaine McLaughlin, R. D.; Douglas Phillips, Phillips Farms; Cindy Avram, Rogers NK Seed Co.; Pat P. Schmidt; and special thanks to Laura Kinkle at the United Fresh Fruit and Vegetable Association for tracking down all my information requests so promptly.

The very talented Jane Reinsel and Connie DeVries are to be credited for assisting with the recipe development as well as with the retesting and perfecting of all recipes.

Thanks to Wardell Parker, Rosi Sandoval, John Anderson, and all the other talented artists at the Mac Access Group in Silver Spring, Maryland, who brought the featured fruits and vegetables to life through their illustrations.

And finally, with special gratitude to my publisher, Hy Steirman, and the wonderful staff at Hastings House for their never ending support, encouragement, and enthusiasm, and making it even better the second time around.

Sandra Conrad Strauss

$\mathcal{J}$NTRODUCTION

This is a book of discovery and exploration. It's designed to introduce the reader to the tantalizing array of some of nature's fanciest fruits and extraordinary vegetables. Included in this cookbook collection is a spirited grouping of some of the very special fruits and vegetables available in most produce departments.

They have strange names like cherimoyas, atemoyas, carambolas, shiitake and enoki mushrooms, rapini, mâche, taro, lychees, feijoas, sapotes, and more. Much of this interest is due to America's increasing love for fresh fruits and vegetables as well as to international influences and ethnic food preferences.

Ethnic cuisines of all types are now firmly rooted in American culture, both at home and in restaurants, and has forever changed the way America cooks and eats. Although some of the fruits and vegetables included in the book are familiar to certain ethnic groups or to specific geographical areas, their virtues have not yet become universally known. For instance, traditional produce items prepared by Hispanic cooks, such as jícama, plantains, tomatillos, and chili peppers, are easily recognized by consumers living in areas with Hispanic populations. Yet seeing these items regularly doesn't automatically suggest they will be sampled.

Geography obviously has a lot to do with familiarity. For example, artichokes are a basic item to West Coast consumers who have the advantage of living close to Castroville, the "artichoke capital of the world." They consider the artichoke a staple, enjoying this sumptuous vegetable as a side dish much like the potato. Likewise, rhubarb is familiar to Midwest consumers. Yet there are millions of consumers across the country interested in how to select, store, and prepare many of the fruits and vegetables available in the produce department. This book should answer most questions.

Some of the fruits and vegetables included in this book were originally classified as "produce exotics," but the term "exotic" can be somewhat intimidating. The industry now generally refers to the more unfamiliar items as "produce specialties."

Some of the produce items in this collection, such as artichokes, kiwifruit, papayas, and mangos, are no longer considered produce specialties as they are usually stocked by supermarkets.

The first edition of this book was published in 1984 after years of experimentation. It was one of the first books to highlight provocative new produce items, published when kiwifruit, snow peas, and even papayas were considered "exotic." This book was written to provide tips about selection, care, serving suggestions, and preparation of these special fruits and vegetables. It is both a cookbook and guide. As a cookbook, it offers new ideas for appetizers, soups, salads, vegetable accompaniments, entrées, beverages, snacks, and desserts, all featuring fresh fruits and vegetables. These fruits have a potential far beyond their traditional usage and can provide a fresh approach to some of your basic recipes.

As a guide, this book answers questions about what to look for and what to avoid, how to store the commodity, how to prepare it, whether it needs to ripen or change color before use, and what parts can be eaten.

As you shop for fresh produce, be on the lookout for new items. Welcome these new fruits and vegetables and they will reward you with some of the freshest and liveliest taste adventures offered by nature.

MAKING IT FAST, EASY, AND NUTRITIOUS: Today there are important needs shaping the way America prepares food—the need for healthful, nutritious meals, the need for quick preparation time, and the need for simplicity. That's why many of the recipes in this collection revolve around these factors. The exceptions are some recipes requiring more preparation time to achieve the most delicious result.

Making it fresh: The natural goodness of the fruits and vegetables featured in this book are complemented by other fresh ingredients. The recipes feature the variety of produce department offerings from apples to zucchini.

Making it fast: Included in this book are many quick-to-fix recipes for main-dish salads, stir-frys, grilled selections, and desserts with a unique twist.

Making it easy: While some fruits and vegetables in this book may be unfamiliar, they're quite easy to prepare. Many fruits and vegetables are the ultimate convenience foods, requiring little preparation.

Making it nutritious: Fresh fruits and vegetables provide more than just great taste. They are nature's original health foods. The National Cancer Institute, the American Heart Association, the U.S. Departments of Agriculture and Health and Human Services, the Surgeon General, and other health authorities and organizations recommend that we eat more fresh fruits and vegetables because of what they contain—fiber, vitamins, and minerals—as well as what they do not have—fat and cholesterol. Fresh fruits and vegetables are also low in sodium or sodium-free.

Nutrition experts recommend that we eat at least five servings of fruits and vegetables daily. This book helps by offering approximately 250 ways to enjoy them!

Making it lighter: Most of the recipes in this book were created with healthful, lighter cooking in mind, but there are some exceptions. I believe every healthful diet is entitled to occasional splurges. While I often use margarine, sometimes butter will create a better result; the same is true for using cream instead of milk. Modify the recipes to suit your personal preferences or health needs.

ARTICHOKE

It has been said that the artichoke is a vegetable of the gods. According to Aegean legend, one of the mythological gods was jealous of a beautiful woman named Cynara. The jealous god transformed Cynara into an artichoke plant, and from then on, artichokes became a delicacy. In Cynara's honor, the artichoke is botanically identified as Cynara scolymus.

Artichokes have been mentioned in literature dating from several centuries before Christ. Actually, what the ancients were eating was a plant called a cardoon, a forefather to the artichoke as we now know it. After the collapse of the Roman Empire, the artichoke disappeared for centuries. During the Renaissance, a modern version of the artichoke was cultivated in Naples, Italy. It was hailed with such gustatory enthusiasm that artichoke aficionados have been lining up ever since for this edible thistle.

Artichokes were introduced to California by Spanish explorers. During the late-nineteenth century, Italian immigrants began planting artichokes along the central California coast. Today, California produces the entire crop of artichokes for U.S. markets.

The artichoke derives its name from the northern Italian words articiocco *and* articoclos, *the latter meaning "a pine cone," in reference to the artichoke's sometimes cone-shaped buds. Artichokes can be spherical, conical, or cylindrical in shape.*

The terms artichoke "heart" and "bottom" are often used interchangeably, but actually they are different parts of the plant. The "heart" is the center of the artichoke, comprised of the pale, inner leaves and the firm-fleshed base. The "bottom" is the succulent, saucer-shaped portion of the artichoke, free of the "choke" and leaves.

AVAILABILITY: Year round, with peak supplies in spring.

SELECTION AND STORAGE: Look for heavy, compact artichokes with tightly clinging leaf scales and a good green color; some varieties are also purplish-red in color. Between winter and early spring, artichokes may be "winter-kissed," showing a bronze tinge that results from frost. This will not affect the quality or flavor. Reject any that are dry or withered.

Size is not an indicator of quality. Artichokes range in size from baby to jumbo and are all mature when picked. Large artichokes are great for stuffing, medium artichokes are perfect for dipping, and "baby" artichokes are well-suited for sautéing, frying, or marinating. Baby artichokes have undeveloped "chokes," so there's no fuzzy choke to remove. When the outer leaves are stripped away, these babies are totally edible.

At home, sprinkle artichokes with a little water and refrigerate in a plastic bag. If purchased in good condition, they can be kept about one week.

PREPARATION: To prepare whole artichokes, slice off about one inch from the top. Trim off the stem so it's even with the base of the artichoke and remove the small, tough leaves surrounding it. If desired, you can trim off any thorny tips from the remaining leaves, but it's not necessary.

Add lemon or lime juice to prevent discoloration during cooking and to enhance flavor; allow 3 tablespoons juice for every quart of water. Water or chicken broth can also be flavored with olive oil, garlic, onions, and herbs.

The fuzzy, inedible centers are easiest to remove after cooking. Carefully spread the leaves apart; pull out the light green and purple-tinged cone to expose the hairy choke. Using a spoon, scrape out the choke to reveal the prized bottom.

To boil: Stand artichokes upright in a large kettle or saucepan and add about 3 inches of water. (See "Preparation" section for additions to cooking liquid.) Cover and cook until a leaf can be easily pulled from the artichoke, about 20–45 minutes depending on size. Drain upside down.

To microwave: The microwave speeds up the preparation time, but can dry out the leaf tips since they do not have much water. They can be easily trimmed after cooking.

To calculate cooking time, count on about half the artichoke's weight for the number of minutes to cook it. For instance, a 12-ounce artichoke should cook in about 6 minutes.

To microwave 1 artichoke, place upside down in a small microwaveable bowl or 10-ounce custard cup. Add 1/4 cup water and a little lemon or lime juice. Cover with wax paper or plastic which has been pricked to allow the steam to escape. Cook on high power, allowing about 6–8 minutes for a 12-ounce artichoke. Then allow to stand covered about 5 minutes to complete the cooking process.

For 2 or more artichokes, place upside down in a deep microwaveable bowl. Add 1 cup water and a little lemon or lime juice. Cover and cook on high power, allowing 8–11 minutes for 2; 14–17 minutes for 4 artichokes; let stand about 5 minutes to complete the cooking.

SERVING SUGGESTIONS:

- Dip leaves and artichoke bottoms into lemon, garlic, or herbed butters or mayonnaise.
- Stuff large artichokes with seafood, cooked poultry, or seasoned bread crumbs and Parmesan cheese.
- Spoon fillings such as mushroom, creamed spinach, or tiny shrimp or crab into large artichoke bottoms.
- Toss cooked baby artichokes into salads or pastas, or serve as an appetizer.

NUTRITION INFORMATION: Artichokes provide potassium, fiber, and a variety of vitamins and minerals. A 12-ounce artichoke (2-ounces edible portion) has about 25 calories.

HOT ARTICHOKE CHEESE DIP

4 artichokes, each about
10 ounces
1¼ cups freshly grated
Parmesan cheese
¼ cup chopped scallions

¾ cup mayonnaise
1 tablespoon fresh lemon or
lime juice
Black pepper
Parsley sprigs

Prepare and cook artichokes according to basic directions. Drain upside down and set aside until cool enough to handle. Remove inner cone and fuzzy choke and discard. Scrape the fleshy portion from the base of the leaves; discard leaves. Coarsely chop artichoke bottoms. Place both in a food processor or blender. Add cheese and scallions; purée until smooth. Blend in mayonnaise, lemon or lime juice, and pepper to taste; mix well.

Place in an ovenproof dish and bake at 350° F for 10 minutes, or until heated through. Garnish with parsley and serve with raw vegetables or crackers.

MAKES ABOUT 2 CUPS

MUSHROOM-STUFFED ARTICHOKES

4 artichokes, each about
  12 ounces
3/4 pound fresh mushrooms
2 tablespoons margarine or
  butter
1/2 cup dry bread crumbs
8 ounces ricotta cheese

2 eggs
2 tablespoons chopped
  fresh parsley
1 teaspoon dried basil
3/4 teaspoon salt
1/3 cup freshly grated
  Parmesan cheese

Prepare and cook artichokes by one of the methods outlined on pages 16–17. Drain upside down. Turn artichokes right side up and remove the inner cone and fuzzy choke.

Wipe mushrooms with a damp cloth, trim stems, and chop mushrooms. Melt the margarine or butter in a medium skillet. Add the mushrooms and sauté for 4–5 minutes. In a large bowl, combine the sautéed mushrooms and crumbs, tossing to mix well. In a small bowl, combine ricotta cheese, eggs, parsley, basil, and salt. Beat until smooth. Pour over mushrooms and mix well.

Spread leaves open around the center of each artichoke. Place about 1/2 cup mushroom filling in each center. Sprinkle filled tops with Parmesan cheese. Place in a lightly oiled baking dish, cover, and bake at 350° F for 30–35 minutes.

MAKES 4 SERVINGS

ARTICHOKES PARMESAN

A lightly seasoned stuffing blended with freshly grated
Parmesan cheese adds zest to the artichokes.

4 artichokes, each about 8
  ounces
4 tablespoons margarine or
  butter
1/4 cup chopped onion
2 cups soft bread crumbs

3/4 cup freshly grated
  Parmesan cheese,
  divided
2 tablespoons fresh lemon
  or lime juice
1 teaspoon dried oregano
  Clarified butter

Prepare and cook artichokes according to basic directions. Drain upside down. When cool enough to handle, remove inner cone and scrape away fuzzy choke.

In a medium saucepan, melt margarine or butter. Add onion and sauté until tender. Add bread crumbs, 1/2 cup cheese, lemon or lime juice, and oregano; mix to combine. Spread leaves open surrounding the artichoke centers. Divide the crumb mixture, placing some in the center of each artichoke. Sprinkle remaining cheese on top. Place in a baking dish and bake at 375° F for 20 minutes. Serve with clarified butter.

MAKES 4 SERVINGS

CHILLED ARTICHOKE AND ASPARAGUS SALAD

4 artichokes, each about 12 ounces
1 pound fresh asparagus
4 tablespoons ground almonds, divided
3 tablespoons fresh lemon juice

1 tablespoon sugar
¹/₂ teaspoon salt
²/₃ cup light cream
1 lemon

Cook artichokes according to one of the methods outlined on pages 16–17. Drain upside down. Chill.

Trim asparagus; cut spears into 2-inch pieces. Place asparagus in a medium saucepan with enough boiling water to cover. Bring to a boil and cook for about 4–6 minutes, or until crisp-tender; drain well and chill.

Remove leaves from cooked artichokes and reserve; discard fuzzy chokes. Thinly slice artichoke bottoms. In a mixing bowl, combine artichoke slices and asparagus. Place almonds in a pie plate and toast in a preheated 400° F oven 3–4 minutes or until golden brown.

In a screw-top jar, combine 2 tablespoons toasted almonds, lemon juice, sugar, and salt. Gradually add cream. Shake to blend. Pour dressing over vegetables.

Arrange artichoke leaves around rims of 4 salad plates. Place vegetable mixture in center and sprinkle with remaining almonds. Cut lemon into thin slices and garnish salads with lemon.

MAKES 4 SERVINGS

BABY ARTICHOKES ITALIANO

*Most baby artichokes have no developed fuzz or fibrous
leaves in the center. Just trim off the tough outer green
leaves and these babies are completely edible.*

³/₄ pound baby artichokes   *3 tablespoons olive oil*
1 lemon   *1 cup chicken stock*
3 garlic cloves

Trim the stems off at the base of each artichoke and cut ¹/₄ inch
from the tops. Halve the artichokes; squeeze lemon juice over the
cut surfaces. Peel and mince the garlic.

   In a large skillet, heat the oil; add the artichokes and garlic.
Sauté 1 minute over medium heat. Add the stock, bring to a boil,
then cover and reduce heat to low. Cook about 10–20 minutes,
depending on size of the "babies." Drain and serve hot, or chill for
use in salads or as a side dish.

MAKES 4 SERVINGS

PASTA WITH MUSHROOM AND ARTICHOKE SAUCE

*Succulent slices of fresh mushrooms and artichoke bottoms
are simmered together in a vegetarian pasta sauce.*

3 artichokes, each about 12
   ounces
2 garlic cloves
1 large onion
1/2 pound fresh mushrooms
2 large fresh tomatoes
3 tablespoons olive oil
15 ounces tomato sauce
6 ounces tomato paste
1/2 cup water

1/4 cup dry red wine
1/2 teaspoon dried basil
1/2 teaspoon dried oregano
   Salt
1 (9-ounce) package fresh
   pasta (spaghetti or
   linguine)
   Freshly grated Parmesan
   cheese

Trim stems from artichokes. Cook artichokes by one of the
methods outlined on pages 16–17. Drain upside down; set aside.

Peel and mince garlic. Peel and slice onion. Wipe mushrooms
with a damp cloth, trim stems, and slice mushrooms. Blanch,
peel, seed, and chop tomatoes.

Heat the oil in a large saucepan. Add garlic and onion; sauté
over medium heat about 4–5 minutes or until onion is tender. Add
mushrooms and sauté 2–3 minutes more.

Remove leaves from artichokes; scrape out the fuzzy chokes
and discard. Thinly slice or coarsely chop the bottoms. Add
artichoke bottoms, tomatoes, tomato sauce, tomato paste, water,
wine, and herbs to the saucepan. Season with salt, if desired.
Cover and simmer for about 1 hour.

Cook pasta according to package directions or boil in a large pot
of boiling water 2–3 minutes, or until al dente. Drain. Ladle sauce
over cooked pasta. Sprinkle with Parmesan cheese, if desired.

MAKES 4 SERVINGS

TARRAGON CHICKEN WITH BABY ARTICHOKES

1 pound baby artichokes
(about 15–20)
1 1/2 pounds boneless,
skinless chicken breasts
Salt and pepper
3/4 pound fresh mushrooms
1 garlic clove
2 tablespoons olive oil
3 tablespoons margarine
or butter

1 tablespoon cornstarch
1/2 cup heavy cream
1/4 cup dry white wine
1/4 cup chicken stock or
broth
1 tablespoon minced fresh
tarragon or 1 teaspoon
dried tarragon
Salt and pepper
Hot, cooked rice

Trim bases of artichokes and about 1/4 inch of the tops. Remove the outer leaves at the base. Place artichokes in a large saucepan of boiling water. Cover and cook over medium heat about 12–15 minutes (check a leaf to make sure it's tender). Drain and set aside.

Slice chicken into thin strips; season with salt and pepper. Wipe mushrooms with a damp cloth, trim stems, and thinly slice mushrooms. Peel and mince garlic. Slice artichokes lengthwise into halves.

Heat the oil in a large skillet. Add the garlic; sauté 30 seconds. Add the chicken; sauté about 4–5 minutes or until chicken is cooked through. Remove chicken with a slotted spoon; set aside.

Pour off drippings. Melt the margarine or butter in the skillet. Add artichokes and mushrooms; sauté about 4–5 minutes. In a bowl, stir together the cornstarch and cream; gradually stir in the wine, chicken stock, and tarragon; pour into skillet. Return chicken to the skillet. Simmer about 3 minutes, stirring constantly until the sauce is thickened. Season with salt and pepper. Serve over hot, cooked rice.

MAKES 4 SERVINGS

$\mathcal{A}$RUGULA

This pungent, spicy green is flavoring salads across America. As a member of the Cruciferae or Mustard family, it takes on some of the same bold, power-packed qualities as its relations such as radish, turnip, and cabbage.

Also known as rocket, arugula is a familiar green to Mediterranean cooks. Having crossed the Atlantic, it lingered for decades in Italian and Greek neighborhoods. Only recently have these radish-like leaves escaped their ethnic domain and begun to enliven salad creations coast-to-coast.

AVAILABILITY: Year round.

SELECTION AND STORAGE: Look for bright, fresh-looking bunches. Arugula is perishable so use within a day or two. At home, wrap the roots in damp paper towels, place in plastic, and refrigerate.

PREPARATION: Wash arugula well, since sand clings tenaciously to its sprigs. Trim roots and any thick stems, then swish in cold water; rinse and repeat. Pat dry and use immediately or chill for later use.

SERVING SUGGESTIONS: Salads, salads, salads! Beyond its salad repertoire, arugula can be prepared as other greens, sautéed or puréed into soups and sauces or wherever a lively, assertive accent is desired.

NUTRITION INFORMATION: Like other dark leafy greens, arugula is an excellent source of vitamins A and C and iron. It has just 23 calories in a 3½-ounce serving.

ARUGULA, RADICCHIO, AND ENDIVE SALAD WITH TOASTED WALNUTS

2 bunches arugula
1 medium head radicchio
2 small heads Belgian
  endive
¼ pound small mushrooms
2 tablespoons olive oil

2 tablespoons walnut oil
2 tablespoons balsamic
  vinegar
3 tablespoons chopped
  walnuts, toasted

Rinse arugula and radicchio; drain and pat dry. Tear into bite-size pieces. Wash endive and separate the leaves. Arrange endive leaves in a circle all around the edge of a serving plate. Wipe mushrooms with a damp cloth, trim stems, and slice. Combine arugula, radicchio, and mushrooms; place in center of plate. In a measuring cup or bowl, combine oils and vinegar; stir to blend. Drizzle over greens. Sprinkle with walnuts.

MAKES 4 SERVINGS

SALAD OF GREENS WITH SESAME SEEDS

3 slices bread
2 tablespoons margarine or
butter
2 tablespoons sesame seeds
1 tablespoon balsamic
vinegar
2 tablespoons olive oil

$^1/_2$ tablespoon seasoned salt
$^1/_4$ teaspoon coarsely ground
pepper
2 bunches arugula
1 bunch romaine lettuce
1 small red onion
$^1/_4$ cup chopped fresh parsley
Croutons

Cut the bread into cubes. Melt margarine or butter in a large skillet. Add bread and sesame seeds and sauté until golden.

In a measuring cup or bowl, combine vinegar, olive oil, salt, and pepper.

At serving time, rinse arugula and romaine; pat dry and tear into bite-size pieces. Peel and chop onion. Combine the arugula, romaine, onion, and parsley. Stir the dressing and pour over the arugula mixture. Toss gently. Add croutons and serve immediately.

MAKES 6 SERVINGS

GINGERED CHICKEN SALAD

4 skinless, boneless chicken
breast halves
Ginger Marinade (see
page 109)
1 large, ripe avocado
$^1/_4$ cup orange juice

2 large navel oranges
2 bunches arugula (about 6
ounces)
3 tablespoons vegetable oil
2 tablespoons slivered
almonds, toasted

Cut chicken into 2-inch × ¹/₂-inch slices and place in an 8-inch-square dish. Prepare Ginger Marinade; pour over chicken and mix until well-coated. Cover and chill for at least 1 hour.

Peel and pit avocado; cut lengthwise into thin wedges. Brush with 1 tablespoon orange juice. Peel oranges; separate into sections. Rinse arugula well and drain. Remove large stems. Combine 1 tablespoon vegetable oil and remaining 3 tablespoons orange juice in a large bowl; mix until well-blended. Add arugula; toss until well-coated. Divide arugula among 4 dinner plates. Arrange avocado and orange sections in a pinwheel design.

Heat 2 tablespoons vegetable oil in a large skillet. Add chicken and marinade. Cook, stirring constantly, until chicken is browned and done. With slotted spoon, remove chicken from skillet. Mound chicken over avocado mixture. Garnish salad with almonds.

MAKES 4 SERVINGS

ASIAN PEARS

The Asian pear is a unique fruit that pairs qualities of two other wonderful fruits. It combines the juiciness of pears with the crispness of apples. Yet the Asian pear is not a hybrid. The tree's original rootstock was brought to the

United States by Chinese prospectors during the Gold Rush.

There are now more than 25 varieties of Asian pears in this country and more than 100 varieties in Japan. Most of the Asian pears sold in the United States are grown in California and the Pacific Northwest.

Although there are many different varieties of Asian pears, they are mostly marketed collectively, simply as Asian pears. This practice is perhaps too simplified, because it doesn't take into account the unique characteristics of each variety. Asian pears vary in their distinctive qualities as do apples and pears. Therefore, what you see marketed as an Asian pear one week may look entirely different the next.

Asian pears vary in size, shape, color, and flavor. They can be petite or large, round or pear-shaped. They can be yellow, green, or gold, and they can be tinged with red or covered with a cinnamon russet. All Asian pears are bursting with juice and have a firm, crisp texture, which can be very sweet or slightly tart. When purchased they are ready to eat and do not require further ripening as do European pears. They store exceptionally well for several months.

AVAILABILITY: Summer through early spring.

SELECTION AND STORAGE: Look for Asian pears from midsummer. Check for a fragrant aroma. Asian pears are hard when ripe, without the typical "give" of other pear varieties. They're ready to eat, so can be enjoyed immediately. Asian pears can be stored in the refrigerator up to a month or more, in either a plastic or paper bag; or at room temperature, uncovered, for about a week.

PREPARATION: Rinse and enjoy them out of hand or slice, seed, and core for other uses. Asian pears remain slightly firm when cooked, so allow a longer cooking time than for other pears.

SERVING SUGGESTIONS:

- Slice chilled fruit into rounds and serve with soft dessert cheese.
- Poach or sauté slices.
- Add sliced or diced fruit to salads.

NUTRITION INFORMATION: Asian pears provide a fair amount of vitamin C, some fiber, and about 60 calories in $3^1/_2$ ounces.

SZECHWAN CHICKEN SALAD WITH CRISP HONEY-SESAME CRESCENTS

This spicy peanut dressing is a flavorful complement to juicy slivers of Asian pears, plums, and chicken.

Szechwan Peanut Dressing
(recipe follows)
Crisp Honey-Sesame
Crescents (recipe follows)
3 Asian pears

3 red or black plums
$1^1/_2$ pounds cooked,
    boneless chicken
    breasts, chilled
6 cups shredded Chinese
    cabbage

Prepare Szechwan Peanut Dressing; set aside. Prepare Honey-Sesame Crescents; set aside.

Cut Asian pears into halves lengthwise, core, and thinly slice. Thinly slice plums. Remove any skin from chicken; thinly slice chicken. Mound about $1^1/_2$ cups shredded cabbage on 4 individual dinner plates. Arrange Asian pears, plums, and chicken over greens. Drizzle with Szechwan Peanut Dressing or pass at serving time. Serve salad with Crisp Honey-Sesame Crescents.

MAKES 4 SERVINGS

SZECHWAN PEANUT DRESSING

$^1/_4$ cup creamy peanut butter
3 tablespoons white wine or cider vinegar
2 tablespoons reduced-sodium soy sauce
2 tablespoons honey

1 tablespoon sesame oil
4 teaspoons water
1 garlic clove, minced
1 teaspoon hot pepper sauce
$^1/_4$ teaspoon cayenne

In a cup, combine all the dressing ingredients; stir well to combine.

MAKES ABOUT $^2/_3$ CUP

CRISP HONEY-SESAME CRESCENTS

$1^1/_2$ tablespoons margarine or butter
$1^1/_2$ tablespoons honey

2 pita breads
2 teaspoons sesame seeds

Melt margarine or butter. Stir in honey and mix well. Split pita bread crosswise, then cut into halves; brush honey mixture over each half. Sprinkle each crescent with $^1/_4$ teaspoon sesame seeds. Place crescents on a baking sheet; bake in a preheated 400° F oven 5 minutes or until golden brown. Remove from oven. Cool slightly. Serve with Szechwan Chicken Salad.

MAKES 8 CRESCENTS

ASIAN PEARS WITH CREAMY ALMOND TOPPING

This almond-flavored sweetened cream cheese garnished with crushed nuts is a delicious complement to crisp chunks of Asian pears—a quick dessert prepared in minutes.

2 tablespoons slivered
    almonds
3 Asian pears
1 tablespoon almond liqueur
3 ounces cream cheese,
    softened

1 tablespoon heavy cream
4 teaspoons sugar
$^1/2$ teaspoon almond extract

Preheat oven to 400° F. Place almonds on a baking sheet and toast about 3–4 minutes or until golden brown. Remove from oven; allow to cool.

Peel, seed, and core Asian pears; cut into bite-size chunks. Place pears in a bowl; drizzle with liqueur and gently toss. Set aside.

In a small mixing bowl, combine cream cheese, heavy cream, sugar, and almond extract. Beat mixture until smooth.

Finely chop almonds. Divide pears among 4 dessert dishes. Top with a dollop of the cream cheese mixture. Garnish with the chopped almonds.

MAKES 4 SERVINGS

POACHED ASIAN PEAR SLICES WITH RASPBERRY SAUCE

Crisp-textured Asian pears are better suited for poaching in slices than as a whole. They are easier to eat this way and just as delicious!

4 Asian pears	1 cinnamon stick
1/2 cup sugar	Raspberry Sauce (recipe
1 cup water	follows)
Juice of 1/2 lemon	

Peel, core, and thinly slice pears. In a large skillet, combine sugar, water, lemon juice, and cinnamon. Bring to a boil; add pears. Cover and simmer 10–15 minutes or until soft (Asian pears retain some of their crispness even after cooking). Remove from heat and chill pears in poaching liquid for several hours.

At serving time, drain pear slices and arrange in a pinwheel design on individual dessert plates and drizzle with some of the chilled Raspberry Sauce.

MAKES 4 SERVINGS

RASPBERRY SAUCE

1 cup fresh raspberries	2 tablespoons sugar
1/3 cup fresh orange juice	2 teaspoons cornstarch

In a small saucepan, combine raspberries, orange juice, sugar, and cornstarch. Bring to a boil and cook 1–2 minutes until sauce is clear and thickened. Remove from heat. Put through a sieve; discard seeds. Cover and chill until serving time.

MAKES 4 SERVINGS

POACHED ASIAN PEAR SLICES
A L'ORANGE

Prepare Poached Asian Pear Slices as above. Chill
Asian pears in poaching liquid. Prepare Orange Sauce,
chill, and serve with Poached Asian Pear Slices.

MAKES 4 SERVINGS

ORANGE SAUCE

2 oranges
$^1/_2$ cup currant jelly
$^1/_3$ cup orange liqueur

$^1/_8$ teaspoon ground
cinnamon
Sweetened heavy cream,
whipped

Cut peel from 1 orange into $^1/_8$-inch thick strips, about 1-inch long. Juice oranges and measure $^1/_2$ cup. Set aside.

In a small saucepan, bring 2 cups water to a boil. Add orange strips; cover and cook for 5 minutes. Drain and reserve.

In a medium saucepan, combine orange juice and jelly. Heat the mixture over low heat until the jelly has melted and the mixture is smooth. Remove from heat. Stir in orange liqueur and cinnamon. Add the reserved orange strips. Chill the sauce until serving.

At serving time, arrange poached pear slices in a pinwheel design on individual dessert plates. Drizzle sauce and some of the orange strips over the pears. Top with a dollop of whipped cream and garnish with a few orange strips.

MAKES 4 SERVINGS

GLAZED ASIAN PEARS WITH TOASTED ALMONDS

Lightly sweetened and sautéed Asian pears are ideal for a fast side dish.

3 Asian pears, about 6–8
ounces each
2 tablespoons margarine or
butter
Juice of ¹/₂ lemon
3 tablespoons sugar

Ground cinnamon
1 tablespoon almond liqueur
2 tablespoons sliced almonds,
toasted

Peel, core, and slice pears. In a large, nonstick skillet, melt margarine or butter. Add pears and squeeze juice of lemon half over pears. Sprinkle with sugar and cinnamon to taste. Sauté 3 minutes over medium-high heat. Remove from heat. Pour liqueur over pears. Transfer to serving dish and garnish with toasted almonds.

MAKES 4 SERVINGS

ATEMOYA AND CHERIMOYA

Custardlike in quality, these two creamy-fleshed fruits are from the same family tree or genus, the Annona. The species originated in South America and later was cultivated in South and Central America, the Caribbean, and tropical regions around the world.

The atemoya is now commercially grown in Florida; the cherimoya in California, South America, Spain, Portugal, Australia, and the French Riviera. Although plantings are increasing for both these fruits, they require delicate cultivation and harvesting techniques as well as special care in shipment, so you can expect to pay a premium for this kid-glove treatment.

These uniquely shaped fruits might appear a bit formidable at first. The atemoya, about the size and shape of a medium artichoke, has a grayish green, leathery exterior with protruding scales. The cherimoya, round or heart-shaped, has a light green skin notched with a medallion design.

The flavor varies from fruit to fruit depending on the variety, but they take on a delicious bouquet of other tropical fruits, with hints of pineapple, papaya, banana, or mango splashed into a vanilla custard!

AVAILABILITY: Atemoyas are generally available from late August through October or November. Cherimoyas can be found from November or December through May.

SELECTION AND STORAGE: Choose fruits of any size, indicating variety rather than maturity. Size doesn't determine quality. Firm fruit requires additional ripening at home. Store fruit at room temperature until the fruit yields to gentle pressure. These fruits can ripen quickly, so check them daily. Refrigerate only when fruit yields to gentle pressure and use promptly after ripening. *

PREPARATION: Both the atemoya's and cherimoya's flesh is dotted with large, black seeds which must be removed. Either cut into halves or peel the skin away in strips.

SERVING SUGGESTIONS: These fruits are so exquisite that they should be prepared very simply to savor their unique tropical allure.

- Halve or quarter fruit, and splash with orange juice.
- Add chunks of atemoya or cherimoya to fruit salads, drizzled with a citrus dressing for tangy accent.
- Purée the custardy flesh and flavor with the zest of orange, lemon, lime, or tangerine. Use in no-bake pies or sherbets.
- Combine fruit purée with sweetened whipped cream and layer parfait-style with other fresh fruits and squares of pound cake.

NUTRITION INFORMATION: A 3½-ounce serving of either fruit provides vitamin C and other nutrients, is free of sodium, and has about 95 calories.

* NOTE: The splitting of the atemoya's stem end and darkening of the skin is natural as it ripens—those are signs of good eating ahead!

CHILLED ATEMOYA AND CITRUS SOUP

1³/₄ pounds atemoya
1 cup fresh orange juice
3 tablespoons sugar
3 tablespoons orange
  liqueur

1 tablespoon fresh lemon
  juice
¹/₂ cup light cream
Fresh mint sprigs or
  thinly sliced orange slices

Peel atemoya and cut into chunks. Carefully remove the seeds, scraping as much of the flesh from the seed as possible. Place chunks in a food processor or blender; purée until smooth. Add orange juice, sugar, liqueur, and lemon juice; whirl until blended. Pour in cream and whirl to blend. Chill until serving time. At serving time, pour into 4 individual dessert bowls. Garnish with mint or orange slices.

MAKES ABOUT 3¹/₂ TO 4 CUPS

CHERIMOYA CREAM AND ORANGE PARFAITS

Puréed cherimoya is accented with orange and layered with a fresh citrus filling for a refreshing and dramatic dessert.

ORANGE FILLING

²/₃ cup sugar
¹/₄ cup cornstarch

2 cups orange juice

CHERIMOYA CREAM

1 1/2 pounds cherimoya
Grated peel from 1
orange
1 tablespoon orange-
flavored liqueur

1 envelope gelatin
1/4 cup water, divided
1/4 cup sugar
1/2 cup heavy cream

In a medium saucepan, combine sugar and cornstarch; mix well. Gradually stir in orange juice. Cook over medium heat until mixture boils, thickens, and becomes translucent. Remove from heat, cover, and chill at least 2 hours (sufficient chilling is needed for proper layering of parfaits).

Meanwhile, prepare Cherimoya Cream. Peel the cherimoya and cut into chunks, removing and discarding seeds. Place cherimoya in a food processor or blender; purée until smooth; measure 1 1/2 cups purée. Stir in orange peel and liqueur; set aside.

In a cup, sprinkle gelatin over 2 tablespoons cold water; set aside. In a small saucepan, combine sugar and remaining 2 tablespoons water. Bring mixture to a boil over medium-high heat; boil 2 minutes. Add gelatin mixture to hot syrup, stirring until dissolved. Stir hot syrup into puréed cherimoya. Cover and chill mixture for at least 1 hour or until Orange Filling is well-chilled.

When both mixtures are well-chilled, whip the cream in a medium mixing bowl. Fold cherimoya mixture into the whipped cream.

Using about 1/2 cup of each mixture per glass, spoon about 1/4 cup of the Cherimoya Cream into 4 parfait glasses, then gently spoon about 1/4 cup of the Orange Filling; repeat layers ending with the Orange Filling topped with a dollop of Cherimoya Cream. Refrigerate until serving time. To serve, garnish with a little orange zest over the Cherimoya Cream, and place a slice of carambola on each rim, if desired.

MAKES 4 SERVINGS

$\mathcal{B}$ELGIAN ENDIVE

The satiny, sleek ivory stalks of Belgian endive convey the message of elegance. This distinctive vegetable has long been revered for its pleasant sharpness.

Also known as witloof, Belgian endive is a member of the chicory family. In the mid-nineteenth century, many Europeans were substituting common chicory roots for imported coffee beans. A Belgian gardener unearthed the white leaves growing from a chicory root in a cellar. These humble "roots" brought Belgian endive to culinary stardom.

Today, its creamy color is obtained by growing endive in the dark, out of sunlight, which naturally bleaches the heads or chicons. Belgium is a major supplier to the U.S. market. With the growing popularity of Belgian endive, the United States and other European countries are also growing this stately vegetable.

Like its relatives curly endive and escarole, Belgian endive has a special, slightly bitter tang, making it a snappy salad choice. Yet it is also a luxurious cooked vegetable served braised, sautéed, or baked. No matter how it's prepared, it provides a crowning touch to any meal.

AVAILABILITY: Year round, with peak supplies November through March.

SELECTION AND STORAGE: Look for tightly furled stalks of creamy white color. The leaves should be pale yellow at the tips. A slight browning along the edges can be removed. The center of the stem end should "give" slightly. When recipes list weight instead of quantity, figure five medium-size endives per pound.

At home, wrap in a paper bag and refrigerate in the vegetable drawer. If stored properly, endives can be kept for a week or longer.

PREPARATION: Separate the leaves or cut crosswise into rounds. Rinse and prepare as needed. Belgian endive should not be cooked in cast iron for this will discolor the leaves. It can be prepared by braising, sautéing, and baking. Belgian endive can also be steamed, boiled, or microwaved.

SERVING SUGGESTIONS:
- Stuff leaves with spiced semi-soft cheese to serve as an appetizer.
- Arrange leaves and orange or tangelo sections in a spoke fashion and drizzle with a vinaigrette.
- Combine with a mixture of leafy greens in salads.
- Its pale leaves are an attractive accent for brightly colored vegetables like red bell pepper or radicchio.
- For steamed, microwaved, or boiled endives try the following extra special touches:

  1. Melt margarine or butter in a skillet then add precooked endives, cooking over medium heat until lightly browned. For extra flavor, stir in minced garlic or shallots during the last few seconds of cooking.
  2. Slice precooked endives into halves lengthwise, sprinkle

with Parmesan cheese, dot with margarine or butter, and broil just until the cheese is golden.

3. For creamy endives, melt margarine or butter in a skillet, then add precooked endives. Sprinkle with lemon juice and season with salt and coarsely ground black pepper. Pour in heavy cream, allowing about 1/4 cup for 4 endives, and roll endives in the cream. Cover and cook about 5 minutes longer.

NUTRITION INFORMATION: Belgian endive contributes vitamin A, some of the B vitamins, other nutrients, and fiber. One leaf is low in sodium and has just 1 calorie.

BRAISED ENDIVES

8 *medium heads of Belgian endive*
4 *tablespoons margarine or butter*
1 *tablespoon lemon juice*
1/4 *cup chicken stock or broth*

1 *teaspoon sugar*
Salt and coarsely ground black pepper
1 *tablespoon chopped fresh parsley*

Rinse endives and pat them dry. Melt the margarine or butter in a large skillet; add endives and sauté over medium-high heat until lightly colored on all sides. Add lemon juice, chicken stock, sugar, and seasonings. Cover and cook over low heat for 30–40 minutes or until tender. Sprinkle with parsley and serve.

MAKES 4 SERVINGS

WATERCRESS-ENDIVE SALAD

2 heads of Belgian endive
1 bunch of watercress
2 medium avocados

Juice of 1 lemon
6 ounces fresh mushrooms
Croutons
Mustard Dressing (recipe follows)

Separate leaves of endive from heads and cut into bite-size pieces. Trim thick stems from watercress and discard. Place greens in a large salad bowl. Peel, pit, and dice the avocado and squeeze the lemon juice over the pieces. Toss to coat avocado thoroughly with lemon juice. Wipe the mushrooms with a damp cloth, trim stems, and slice the mushrooms. Combine avocado and mushrooms with the salad greens.

MUSTARD DRESSING

3 tablespoons fresh lemon juice
2 tablespoons white wine vinegar

2 teaspoons Dijon mustard
1 garlic clove
$1/2$ cup corn oil
$1/8$ teaspoon black pepper

In a screw-top jar, combine lemon juice, vinegar, mustard, and garlic. Shake well. Add oil and pepper and shake vigorously. Pour dressing over salad right before serving and toss to coat. Garnish with croutons.

MAKES 4 SERVINGS

APPLE, WALNUT, AND ENDIVE SALAD

¹/₄ cup fresh lemon juice
3 tablespoons vegetable oil
2 tablespoons honey
¹/₄ teaspoon Dijon mustard

4 heads of Belgian endives
2 medium red apples
¹/₄ cup chopped walnuts

In a screw-top jar, combine the lemon juice, oil, honey, and mustard. Shake well and set aside.

Rinse and core endives; pat dry with paper towels. Separate leaves and cut 2 heads into thin slices. Arrange leaves of 2 remaining endives around rim of serving plate. Core, seed, and dice the apples. In a salad bowl combine sliced endives, apples, and walnuts. Pour dressing over salad. Toss to coat. Mound salad in center of endive-rimmed serving plate.

MAKES 4 SERVINGS

$\mathcal{B}$OK CHOY

This popular Oriental vegetable resembles the American garden favorite Swiss chard, and so is sometimes referred to as Chinese chard. It is also known as pak choi, Chinese mustard cabbage, and Chinese white cabbage. As a mem-

ber of the Brassica species, it shares some traits with its cabbage relatives and so is sometimes marketed as "Chinese cabbage."

Bok choy has some distinctive qualities. This Oriental delicacy has thick, white, rounded stalks topped with broad, dark green leaves. The crisp-textured, juicy ribs have a light, delicate flavor, and the leaves are soft with a mild, cabbage flavor.

AVAILABILITY: Year round.

SELECTION AND STORAGE: Look for bok choy with bright white stalks and glossy, fresh-looking leaves. Store in a plastic bag in the refrigerator and use within a few days.

PREPARATION: Wash and separate the leaves from the stalks. Cut or tear leaves and slice the stalks. Bok choy can be eaten raw, but cooking enhances its flavor. When preparing bok choy, keep cooking time to a minimum, adding the leaves during the last minutes of cooking.

"Baby bok choy" can be served whole or halved and quartered.

To stir-fry: For 5 cups of sliced stalks and shredded leaves, heat 2 tablespoons vegetable oil with minced fresh garlic. Stir-fry stalks for less than 1 minute; add 2 tablespoons water, chicken stock, or a combination of soy sauce and water. Cover and cook a few more minutes until crisp tender. Add the leaves and stir-fry just until wilted.

To boil: Place the stalks from one large head of bok choy (or 1 1/4–1 1/2 pounds) in a large skillet. Pour in 1/4 inch water, cover, and cook for about 2 minutes. Add the leaves, cover, and continue cooking about 1–2 more minutes or until the leaves wilt. Drain and season to taste.

To microwave: Place the stalks from a large head of bok choy (or 1¼–1½ pounds) in a 2-quart microwaveable container. Add 2 tablespoons water, cover, and microwave on high power for 3 minutes. Stir in the leaves, cover, and microwave a few more minutes. Allow to stand about 2 minutes. The stalks should be tender when pierced and the leaves wilted.

SERVING SUGGESTIONS:

- Season hot, cooked bok choy with margarine, soy sauce, minced gingerroot, or toasted sesame seeds.
- Add to stir-fry recipes.
- Add thinly sliced ribbons of leaves to Oriental-style soups.
- Drizzle a soy vinaigrette over hot, cooked bok choy.

NUTRITION INFORMATION: A ½-cup serving provides vitamins A and C, calcium, other nutrients, and has about 15 calories.

BEEF WITH BOK CHOY AND SHIITAKE MUSHROOMS IN OYSTER SAUCE

¾ pound flank steak or sirloin

3 garlic cloves

2 tablespoons water

1 tablespoon dry sherry or sake

1 tablespoon reduced-sodium soy sauce

½ teaspoon sugar

1 tablespoon plus 2 teaspoons cornstarch, divided

2½ tablespoons peanut oil, divided

2 tablespoons bottled oyster sauce

½ cup chicken broth or stock

1 pound bok choy (about 6 ribs)

4 ounces fresh shiitake mushrooms

Cut beef with the grain into 1 1/2-inch wide strips, then cut across the grain into 1/8-inch thick slices. Peel and mince garlic. In a medium bowl, combine garlic, water, sherry, soy sauce, sugar, and 2 teaspoons cornstarch; mix well. Stir in 1/2 tablespoon oil. Add beef, toss to coat with the mixture; allow to marinate for 15 minutes.

Meanwhile in a cup, mix together oyster sauce and 1 tablespoon cornstarch; stir in chicken broth. Set mixture aside.

Cut bok choy leaves from ribs. Cut ribs diagonally into 1/4-inch slices; coarsely shred leaves. Set aside ribs and leaves separately. Wipe mushrooms with a damp cloth. Cut caps into about 1/4-inch slices; thinly slice stems. Set vegetables aside.

Heat 1 tablespoon oil in a large skillet or wok. Add the bias-cut bok choy slices and stir-fry over medium-high heat for 1 minute. Add mushrooms and sauté vegetables 1 minute. Remove vegetables from wok; set aside.

Heat remaining 1 tablespoon oil. Add meat, stir-frying over medium-high heat about 2 minutes or until browned. Add bok choy leaves and return cooked vegetables to skillet or wok. Stir in sauce, stirring until sauce boils and thickens.

MAKES 4 SERVINGS

SUKIYAKI

Bok choy is featured in this popular Japanese recipe. In-gredients are traditionally arranged on a platter and cooked at tableside.

2 ounces cellophane
   noodles
1 pound beef tenderloin
^{1}/2 cup sake or dry sherry
^{1}/2 cup beef broth
^{1}/4 cup reduced-sodium soy
   sauce
^{1}/4 cup water

3 tablespoons sugar
6 bok choy ribs
4 ounces fresh shiitake
   mushrooms
6 scallions
1 tablespoon peanut or
   vegetable oil

Soak noodles in cold water for 30 minutes to rehydrate. Slice beef very thinly, cutting across the grain. Place in a medium bowl. Combine sake or sherry, broth, soy sauce, water, and sugar; pour mixture over beef. Set aside while preparing vegetables.

Cut the bok choy leaves from the ribs and shred the leaves; cut the ribs into ^{1}/4-inch diagonal slices. Wipe mushrooms, quarter the caps, and thinly slice the stems. Cut scallions into 1^1/2- to 2-inch lengths. Drain noodles; arrange noodles and vegetables on a large platter.

In a wok or large skillet, heat the oil. Remove the beef from the broth mixture using a slotted spoon. Add the beef and cook over medium-high heat until slightly pink. Remove beef; set aside and pour off drippings.

Add broth mixture to wok and bring to a boil. If using a wok, place the bok choy ribs, mushrooms, and noodles in separate areas of the wok; do not mix. Simmer uncovered for 1 minute. Add the bok choy leaves and scallions; return beef to wok and cook 1 more minute. Serve immediately in separate areas of the plate.

MAKES 4 SERVINGS

SHRIMP SAUTÉ WITH BOK CHOY, MUSHROOMS, AND SPROUTS

1 pound large, raw shrimp
1 garlic clove
2 large carrots
1/2 pound fresh mushrooms
5 bok choy ribs, including leaves
1 cup fresh bean sprouts

1/2 cup chicken stock or broth
4 teaspoons cornstarch
1 teaspoon reduced-sodium soy sauce
3 tablespoons peanut or vegetable oil, divided

Peel and devein the shrimp; cut crosswise into halves and set aside.

Peel and mince garlic. Peel carrots and cut diagonally into thin slices. Wipe the mushrooms with a damp cloth, trim the stems, and slice. Cut bok choy ribs into 1/4-inch bias-cut slices and the leaves into 1/2-inch strips. Rinse sprouts, drain, and pat dry.

In a cup, gradually stir chicken stock into cornstarch; add soy sauce and set aside.

Heat 2 tablespoons oil in a large skillet or wok. Add shrimp and garlic; sauté for 3–4 minutes or until shrimp is opaque and cooked through. Remove shrimp with a slotted spoon; set aside.

Heat remaining 1 tablespoon oil. Add carrots and mushrooms; sauté over medium-high heat for 3 minutes. Add the bok choy ribs and sauté 1 minute, then stir in bok choy leaves and sprouts; cook 1 more minute. Return shrimp to skillet or wok. Pour sauce mixture over shrimp and vegetables, cooking just until thickened, stirring constantly.

MAKES **4** SERVINGS

CACTUS PEAR

The refreshing, colorful cactus pear (also known as the prickly pear, barbary fig, Indian pear, and Indian fig) is the fruit of several varieties of the Opuntia *cactus. This queen of desert fruits is native to the Americas, but the popularity of the cactus pear has spread worldwide.*

Most supplies in the United States are grown in the Southwest and Mexico, with additional cultivation in Spain, Italy, and Israel to supply further world demand.

This fruit is barrel to pear-shaped with flesh reminiscent of watermelon in both its texture and sweet flavor. The skin color of the most commonly found varieties range from olive green to burgundy, although they can be yellowish or light green as well. The interior of this thorny delicacy is strikingly brilliant—fuschia, crimson, rose, yellowish-orange, or even chartreuse, depending on the variety.

Botanically, the cactus pear is actually a berry, which explains the plethora of seeds! The flesh is dotted with rather tough seeds, some of which are a bit unyielding and are best discarded.

AVAILABILITY: Peak availability is August through December, with limited supplies through spring.

SELECTION AND STORAGE: Select cactus pears that are firm, but tender with a bright, fresh appearance. They should be kept at room temperature until they are soft, then refrigerated. Refrigeration is not required but aids in prolonged storage. If refrigerated, cactus pears should keep for a week or more.

PREPARATION: The sharp spines are mechanically removed from cactus pears prior to marketing, but some inevitably remain and can be irritating to the skin. To avoid this thorny problem, spear the fruit with a fork and cut off about $^1/2$ inch from each end. Slit the skin lengthwise, and slip the tip of a knife under each slit. Then pull the skin down using a knife blade or, for easier peeling, your fingers.

To purée, scoop the pulp into a blender or food processor and process. Place purée through a strainer to remove any seeds or strings. One large cactus pear yields about $^1/4$ cup purée.

SERVING SUGGESTIONS:

- Serve chilled fruit sprinkled with lemon or lime juice.
- Add cactus pear slices or chunks to salads.
- For a light dessert, sprinkle slices lightly with sugar and lemon or lime juice, and top with yogurt or sweetened whipped cream.
- Purée and strain the sauce to use in beverages, sauces, and sorbets.

NUTRITION INFORMATION: A $3^1/2$-ounce serving is a good source of vitamin C and contains about 60 calories.

CREAMY CACTUS COOLER

4 cactus pears
1 banana

$^1/_2$ cup light cream or
    evaporated milk
6–8 ice cubes

Peel the cactus pears. In a blender or food processor, purée pears and strain to remove seeds. Combine puréed pears, banana, light cream, and ice cubes; blend until smooth. Pour into glasses.

MAKES 2 SERVINGS

CALABAZA

The bright orange-fleshed calabaza (kah-la-BAH-sa) is a member of the colorful squash family. It is a hard-shelled squash, commonly, although incorrectly, grouped as a "winter squash," since they are available year round.

Calabazas are round or pear-shaped. They can be as small as a honeydew, but more frequently are much larger and usually marketed in large crescents or chunks. The calabaza has a mottled skin, speckled or streaked with yellow, green, and/or butternut.

Native to the Americas, calabaza has been a culinary

mainstay throughout Central and South America and the Caribbean. Now, with the increasing Latin population in the U.S., it is appearing more regularly in many markets.

AVAILABILITY: Year round.

SELECTION AND STORAGE: When purchasing chunks, look for a close-grained flesh which should be dry like the flesh of other winter squashes. If purchasing whole, check the stem end for soft or moldy spots and select squash with a dull rind. Whole squashes can be stored for a month or more if kept in a cool, dry, well-ventilated area. Cut sections should be refrigerated in plastic and used within a week.

PREPARATION: Split the squash using a large knife. Scoop out the seeds and fibers (saving seeds, if desired, for toasting). Then cut into large chunks. Calabaza can be cooked like other winter squashes, but microwaving is the fastest and easiest technique for cooking large sections or squashes.

To microwave: Place squash chunks in a large, microwaveable dish and cover with wax paper. Cook on high power for 15–18 minutes or until soft, rotating halfway through cooking. Remove from microwave and allow to stand at least 5 minutes to finish cooking. Then scoop out flesh from shell.

To bake: Cut squash into halves and scoop out seeds and fibers. Place cut side down on a rimmed cookie sheet, and add 1/4 cup water. Bake at 375° F about 40–60 minutes or until squash is tender when pierced with a fork. Add more water if needed during cooking.

SERVING SUGGESTIONS:

- Calabaza is best when cooked with other ingredients or mashed or puréed.
- Add chunks to soups or stews; purée into soups.

- Use puréed or mashed calabaza in cakes, pies, puddings, mousses, or quick breads.
- Whole calabazas can be hollowed out and used as a tureen for soups and stews.

NUTRITION INFORMATION: As other hard-shelled squashes, calabaza is an excellent source of vitamins A and C, provides potassium and other nutrients, is low in sodium, and has 35 calories in a $3^1/_2$-ounce portion.

SPICED CALABAZA SOUP

Calabaza, like other hard-shelled squashes, cooks easily in the microwave for this fast-to-fix soup.

3 pounds calabaza	2 tablespoons brown sugar
2 tablespoons margarine or butter	$^1/_4$ teaspoon ground cinnamon
$^3/_4$ cup chopped onion	$^1/_4$ teaspoon ground ginger
$^3/_4$ cup chopped onion	$^1/_4$ teaspoon ground nutmeg
2 cups chicken broth	4 tablespoons heavy cream
1 cup milk or light cream	

Cut squash into halves; discard seeds and fibers. Cut squash into large chunks. Prepare as directed for microwaving calabaza. (See page 53.)

Melt margarine or butter in a large saucepan. Add onion and sauté over medium heat about 4–5 minutes or until tender.

Scrape cooked squash pulp from shell and place in a food processor with the onion. Purée mixture until smooth. Place squash purée in the saucepan. Stir in broth, milk, brown sugar, and spices; mix well. Cook over medium heat until heated through. Ladle into bowls. Carefully dip a tablespoon of cream into the center of each bowl and swirl to form a design.

MAKES 4 SERVINGS

CARAMBOLA

The carambola is a dazzling star in the produce department constellation. Golden yellow when ripe, this glossy, glamorous fruit has five "wings" or ribs which reveal a star-shaped pattern when cut crosswise (hence the nickname starfruit). Its flesh is juicy and translucent, and preparation is exceptionally easy.

Varieties can be sweet, tart, or a combination of both. However, the sweet varieties are currently becoming more dominant. A sweet carambola has a definite citrus quality with a fragrant, flowery accent. Tart varieties taste more like a lemon, but with a fruitier flavor.

The variety may not always be identified for consumers, so check the width of the ribs as a general guide. Sweet varieties often have thicker, wider ribs, while tart varieties have very narrow ribs. Note that there are many different carambola varieties, so this may not be a totally foolproof means of distinguishing between the tart and sweet types.

AVAILABILITY: August to mid-March.

SELECTION AND STORAGE: Green or green-tinged fruits should be stored at room temperature until they turn golden and have developed a fragrant aroma. When fully ripe, they can be refrigerated up to two weeks, if purchased in good condition.

PREPARATION: Carambolas are a no-fuss fruit, requiring no peeling. Just wash and slice, discarding any seeds. The tiny, brown stripe running down the ribs of a ripe carambola can be easily scraped away, if desired.

SERVING SUGGESTIONS:

- Garnish entrées and desserts with star-shaped slices.
- Float slices in beverages, punch bowls, and sparkling water.
- Add slices to fruit, mixed green salads, or poultry salads.
- Sauté with shrimp or scallops.
- Purée into ices or sherbets.

NUTRITION INFORMATION: A medium carambola is an excellent source of vitamin C and has about 40 calories.

CARAMBOLA ORANGE SAUCE

A quick and elegant sauce for poultry, ham, or pork.

2 medium carambolas	1/4 cup sugar
2/3 cup fresh orange juice	1 tablespoon cornstarch

Cut carambolas crosswise into 1/8-inch thick slices; set aside. In a small, microwaveable bowl, combine orange juice, sugar, and cornstarch; mix well. Cover and cook on high power for 2 minutes. Add carambola and cook uncovered about 2–3 minutes more until sauce is translucent. Allow to cool about 15 minutes before serving. At serving time, spoon about ¹/₄ cup sauce over poultry, pork, or slices of ham, arranging carambola over poultry or meat.

MAKES ABOUT 1 CUP (ENOUGH FOR 4 SERVINGS)

STARFRUIT, STRAWBERRY, SHRIMP, AND SPINACH SALAD WITH STRAWBERRY VINAIGRETTE

³/₄ *pound fresh spinach*
2 *small to medium carambolas*
2 *cups sliced fresh strawberries*

³/₄ *pound medium shrimp, cooked, chilled, peeled and deveined*
Strawberry Vinaigrette (recipe follows)

Rinse spinach well and drain. Remove stems and tear leaves into bite-size pieces. Divide spinach among individual salad plates. Thinly slice carambolas. Arrange carambola, strawberries, and shrimp over spinach. Drizzle Strawberry Vinaigrette over salad and serve immediately.

MAKES 4 MAIN-DISH SERVINGS

STRAWBERRY VINAIGRETTE

¹/₂ *cup vegetable oil*
¹/₄ *cup strawberry vinegar*
2 *tablespoons sugar*
¹/₂ *teaspoon salt*

¹/₂ *teaspoon paprika*
2 *tablespoons chopped scallion*

Combine ingredients in a screw-top jar. Shake well to blend.

MAKES 1 CUP

FRESH FRUIT WITH HONEY-LIME YOGURT DRESSING

$^1/_2$ medium honeydew melon
2 medium carambolas
2 kiwifruit
1 cup sliced strawberries
  Sugar (optional)

8 ounces vanilla yogurt
1 large lime
2 tablespoons honey
  Watercress sprigs (optional)

Scoop seeds from melon; thinly slice melon and cut wedges crosswise into halves. Cut carambolas crosswise into $^1/_8$-inch slices. Peel and thinly slice kiwifruit; cut slices into halves. Sprinkle a little sugar over carambola and strawberries, if desired.

On 4 salad plates, arrange honeydew slices in a pinwheel design. Place carambola slices over honeydew slices in the center forming a circle, then mound about $^1/_4$ cup sliced strawberries in the center. Place kiwi in between honeydew wedges.

Spoon yogurt into a small bowl. Grate the peel from the lime and squeeze 2 tablespoons lime juice. Add the lime peel, juice, and honey; stir to combine. To serve, spoon about 3 tablespoons of the honey-lime yogurt dressing over each salad. Garnish with sprigs of watercress, if desired.

MAKES 4 SERVINGS

GINGERED SHRIMP WITH CARAMBOLA AND VEGETABLES

1 pound medium shrimp
1/2 cup water
3 tablespoons fresh lemon juice
3 tablespoons reduced-sodium soy sauce
2 tablespoons honey
1 tablespoon dry white wine
1 1/2 teaspoons minced, fresh ginger

1 garlic clove, minced
1 medium carambola
1 medium red bell pepper
1/4 pound fresh snow peas or sugar snap peas
3 scallions
1 1/2 teaspoons cornstarch
2 tablespoons peanut oil

Peel and devein shrimp; place in a shallow bowl. In a measuring cup, combine water, lemon juice, soy sauce, honey, wine, ginger, and garlic; mix well. Pour 1/2 cup marinade over the shrimp, reserving remainder for final sauce. Cover shrimp and refrigerate; set aside.

To prepare for cooking, cut carambola crosswise into 1/8-inch slices. Remove membrane and seeds from bell pepper; cut into 1-inch pieces. Trim snow peas or sugar snap peas. Bias-cut scallions into 1-inch lengths. Set aside.

Drain and discard marinade from shrimp. Stir cornstarch into the reserved marinade; mix well. In a large skillet, heat oil. Add pepper; sauté 1 minute. Add shrimp and cook 2 minutes longer or until opaque. Add carambolas, snow peas or sugar snap peas, and reserved ginger sauce, cooking just until the sauce thickens. Stir in the scallions and serve immediately.

MAKES 4 SERVINGS

CELERIAC

Celeriac (pronounced se-ler-ē-ak) is a vegetable of many identities. It is also known as celery root, celery knob, and turnip-rooted celery. Naturally, all of these names reinforce its close relationship to celery. However, unlike celery, its stalks are not eaten; celeriac is prized for its root.

Celeriac is an unlikely candidate for any glamorous vegetable award. It is an irregularly shaped sphere, usually 2–4 inches in diameter, with a coarse, brown skin and tiny rootlets protruding from the globe.

Celeriac probably originated around the Mediterranean. Although traditionally it has been popular with European cooks, this gnarled vegetable is also grown in home gardens and has been available in markets in the United States since the beginning of the nineteenth century.

American palates are perhaps most familiar with celeriac served as the French hors d'oeuvre, Céleri-rave ré-moulade, a tangy creation of julienne slices of celeriac, either raw or lightly blanched, marinated in a rémoulade sauce.

Additionally, it offers culinary interest served as a hot vegetable alone or in combination with others, simmered in soups or stews, or cooked and puréed with potatoes.

AVAILABILITY: September through April.

SELECTION AND STORAGE: Look for small to medium-size roots, up to one pound; larger ones tend to be woody or hollow with pithy centers. If tops are attached, they should be green and fresh-looking. Avoid any knobs that are soft. Trim off any tops or long roots which may still be attached at the base before storing. The tops can be used in soups and stews, but they are far more powerful in flavor than celery. Refrigerate celeriac in plastic and use within a week.

PREPARATION: Celeriac darkens or oxidizes quickly once cut or when the surface is exposed to air from peeling. Therefore, to reduce discoloration, be sure to plunge cut or peeled celeriac immediately into cool water to which a little lemon juice has been added. Due to the thickness of the skin and gnarled surface, peeling is easier with a paring knife rather than with a peeler. Once peeled, celeriac can be sliced, diced, shredded, or julienned.

To cook sliced or diced celeriac, cover with 1 inch of boiling water and boil, allowing 8–10 minutes for $^1/_2$- to 1-inch slices, 5–8 minutes for $^1/_2$-inch cubes, or until tender. Celeriac can turn mushy, so check it frequently while cooking.

To microwave a one pound celeriac, pierce the skin several times, then cook on high power 8–10 minutes or just until tender. Allow about 10 minutes cooking time if you're planning to purée the celeriac.

SERVING SUGGESTIONS:

- For marinated salads, shredded or julienned, raw or slightly blanched, and dressed with a vinaigrette, mayonnaise, or cream dressing.
- Purée cooked celeriac alone or with cooked potatoes.

- Layer cooked celeriac slices in a buttered or lightly oiled baking pan, and arrange apple slices over the celeriac. Sprinkle with brown sugar and dot with margarine or butter. Bake at 350° F for about 30 minutes or microwave until tender.
- Add celeriac chunks to soups and stews.
- Serve celeriac either creamed or in gratins.
- Drizzle cooked slices or chunks with melted margarine or butter seasoned with dill or tarragon.

NUTRITION INFORMATION: A 3½-ounce portion provides vitamin C, potassium, and other minerals, and has about 25 calories.

CÉLERI-RAVE RÉMOULADE

2 teaspoons Dijon mustard
1 egg yolk
½ teaspoon fresh lemon juice
¼ teaspoon salt
⅓ cup vegetable oil
2 tablespoons light cream

2 teaspoons fresh minced tarragon or ½ teaspoon dried tarragon
1 pound celeriac
1 tablespoon fresh lemon juice or vinegar

In a medium mixing bowl, mix the mustard, egg yolk, lemon juice, and salt together. Gradually add the oil in a thin stream, beating vigorously. Stir in the cream and tarragon. Set aside.

Peel and shred the celeriac. Place celeriac in enough boiling water to cover to which lemon juice or vinegar has been added. Cook for 1 minute. Drain immediately in a colander and rinse with cold water. Pat dry with paper toweling.

Combine celeriac with reserved dressing. Toss to coat. Chill well before serving.

MAKES 4 SERVINGS

CHUNKY BEEF AND VEGETABLE SOUP

2 pounds beef shanks
Black pepper
2 tablespoons vegetable oil
2 large onions
2 garlic cloves
4 medium carrots

1/4 cup chopped fresh parsley
2 quarts beef stock
1 pound celeriac
Croutons
Freshly grated Parmesan
cheese

Season the beef with pepper. In a large kettle, heat the oil. Add the meat and brown well. Peel and slice the onions. Peel and mince the garlic. Push meat along the sides of the pan. Add the onions and garlic and cook until onion is translucent. Peel the carrots and cut into 1/2-inch pieces. Combine carrots, parsley, and beef stock with the beef and onions. Cover and simmer over low heat for about 1 1/2 hours.

Remove the meat and allow to cool slightly. Cut the meat into bite-size chunks, discarding fat and bones. Return meat to the soup. Peel and dice the celeriac. Add to soup and cook for 15 minutes more, or until celeriac is tender. To serve, top with croutons and sprinkle with Parmesan cheese.

MAKES 6 TO 8 SERVINGS

CARROT-CELERIAC SALAD

3 medium carrots
1 pound celeriac
2 tablespoons fresh lemon
  juice

$^1/_4$ cup chopped onion
$^1/_2$ cup mayonnaise
Salt

Peel and shred carrots and celeriac and place in a mixing bowl. Sprinkle lemon juice over vegetables and toss. Add onion, mayonnaise, and salt to taste. Toss to coat. Cover and chill for at least 1 hour.

MAKES 4 SERVINGS

CELERIAC SALAD WITH HONEY-YOGURT DRESSING

1 pound celeriac
  Juice of $^1/_2$ lemon
1 large red apple
$^1/_3$ cup raisins

$^1/_3$ cup chopped walnuts
1 cup plain yogurt
2 tablespoons honey

Peel and shred celeriac. Measure enough to equal about 2 cups, and place in a medium mixing bowl. Squeeze lemon juice over celeriac and toss. Core, seed, and chop the apple. Add apple, raisins, and walnuts to celeriac. Mix together yogurt and honey and pour over apple-celeriac mixture. Toss to coat. Cover and chill.

MAKES 4 SERVINGS

LAMB STEW WITH CELERIAC

1 1/2 *pounds boneless lamb*	3 *tablespoons vegetable oil*
1/4 *cup flour*	1 *quart water*
1 *teaspoon salt*	6 *medium carrots*
1/4 *teaspoon pepper*	1 *pound celeriac*
3 *garlic cloves*	1 *tablespoon Worcestershire*
2 *medium onions*	*sauce*

Trim fat from lamb and cut meat into 1-inch cubes. Combine flour, salt, and pepper in a mixing bowl and coat the lamb with the mixture; reserve excess flour.

Peel and mince garlic. Peel onions and cut into wedges. Heat oil in a large kettle. Add garlic and lamb; brown meat on all sides over medium heat. Add onions and cook about 5 minutes or until onions are tender. Place remaining flour in a bowl and gradually stir in the water; pour into kettle. Simmer covered, stirring occasionally, for about 1 1/2 hours or until meat is tender.

Peel carrots and celeriac; cut into bite-size chunks. Add vegetables and Worcestershire sauce; simmer covered for 15–20 minutes, or until the vegetables are tender.

MAKES 4 TO 6 SERVINGS

CHAYOTE

Chayote pronounced (chy-o-tay) is a crisp, firm-textured vegetable, a fusion between a cucumber and a zucchini in both texture and flavor. It is a member of the gourd family and was cultivated by the ancient Aztecs and Mayans. Spanish explorers to the New World returned to Europe with it and introduced chayote to Asians.

Today it is widely cultivated in tropical and subtropical regions around the world, including the West Indies, Central and South America, Mexico, New Zealand, Australia, North Africa, and the United States. In other countries, it is known as christophene, chocho, pepinella, and brionne. In the United States, chayotes are commercially grown in the Southwest, Florida, and Louisiana (where it is marketed as mirliton).

There are different varieties of chayote available worldwide, ranging in color, size, and shape. The ones chiefly marketed in the United States are light green or yellow green, although some are dark green or yellowish-white. They are usually pear-shaped, but some are more rounded. The chayote's skin can be smooth or deeply furrowed, and it may even have some prickly spines. They range in weight from ¹/₂–1 pound.

The flat, elliptical seed is edible after cooking; it has a mild-nutlike flavor and a smooth, pliable texture.

AVAILABILITY: Year round, with peak supplies from the fall through spring.

SELECTION AND STORAGE: Choose firm, fresh-looking chayotes. They can be kept in the refrigerator, lightly wrapped, for several weeks.

PREPARATION: Chayote halves can be cooked in a skillet in about 2 inches of boiling water. They should be tender within 25–35 minutes. Chayote slices, cut ¼-inch thick, cooked in ½ inch of water, will cook in 7–9 minutes.

Peeling is generally required, unless the chayotes are very small, and is especially needed for those bearing tiny spines.

SERVING SUGGESTIONS:

- Steam or sauté peeled, sliced, or julienned chayote, and season with fresh herbs and a squeeze of lemon or lime juice.
- Stuff halves with fresh vegetable, poultry, or meat combinations and serve as a main dish.
- Marinate chayote chunks or slices in a vinaigrette with other fresh vegetables and serve as a salad.
- Add chayote slices to soups or stews.

NUTRITION INFORMATION: A 3½-ounce serving provides vitamin C, potassium, and other minerals, and has about 25 calories.

CRISP CHAYOTE STRIPS WITH CREAMY CILANTRO DIP

The chayote's firm texture is ideal for this appetizer.
These crispy, golden brown strips are great by themselves
or served with the dip.

1 chayote, about 12 ounces	1 cup cornflake crumbs
1/3 cup flour	1/3 cup vegetable oil
1 egg or 2 egg whites	Salt
1 tablespoon milk	

Peel chayote and cut into halves; remove seeds. Cut chayote into 1/4-inch strips. Roll strips in flour. Beat the egg or egg whites with the milk. Dip slices into egg mixture, then roll in crumbs.

Heat oil in a large skillet. Cook strips over medium-high heat 3–4 minutes, until golden brown. Drain on paper towels. Season with salt. Serve hot with Creamy Cilantro Dip.

MAKES 4 SERVINGS

CREAMY CILANTRO DIP

1/2 cup dairy sour cream or plain yogurt	1 teaspoon fresh lime juice
1/2 cup mayonnaise	1/2 teaspoon ground cumin
2 tablespoons minced fresh cilantro	Dash cayenne pepper
1 garlic clove, minced	Salt and coarsely ground pepper

Combine ingredients in a bowl. Season with salt and pepper.

MAKES 1 CUP

MARINATED CHAYOTE-BEAN SALAD

2 chayotes, each about 12 ounces
3/4 pound fresh green beans
1 small onion
1/3 cup olive or vegetable oil
1/4 cup white wine vinegar
Juice of 1/2 lime
2 teaspoons minced, fresh tarragon or 1/2 teaspoon dried tarragon
1/4 teaspoon sugar
1/4 teaspoon salt
1/8 teaspoon black pepper
2 medium tomatoes
Lettuce leaves

Peel chayotes, discard the seeds, and cut into thin slices. Trim the green beans and cut into 1-inch lengths. In a large saucepan, cook chayotes and beans in boiling water for about 5 minutes. Drain the vegetables. Peel and chop the onion. Place the vegetables in a large mixing bowl.

In a screw-top jar, combine the oil, vinegar, lime juice, tarragon, sugar, salt, and pepper; shake to mix. Pour the dressing over the vegetables. Cover and chill to marinate.

At serving time cut the tomatoes into wedges and add them to the marinated salad. Arrange the salad on plates lined with lettuce leaves.

MAKES 6 SERVINGS

CHILI PEPPERS

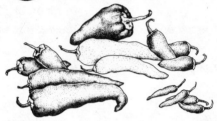

*The spirited chili or capsicum peppers, famous for enliven-
ing cuisines around the world, are being discovered by more
cooks for adding bold, sometimes fiery heat to their culinary
creations.*

*Chili peppers are believed to have originated in Mexico
around 7000 B.C. Christopher Columbus is credited with
discovering the capsicum during his expedition to the West
Indies in search of the Piper nigrum variety of peppers.
The peppercorns from the Piper nigrum variety were used
during the fifteenth century both to flavor and disguise
spoiled meat. Instead Columbus returned to Europe with
the capsicum peppers in hand, a discovery which changed
the course of cuisines around the world.*

*With the popularity of Mexican and Southwestern cui-
sines, chili peppers are acquiring more aficionados. Due to
increasing demand for chili peppers, there is now a rainbow
of chili varieties available in many produce departments.*

*The "heat" in chili peppers varies, even among the same
variety. In fact, the heat can vary with chili peppers from
the same plant. The following descriptions can be useful in
selecting the chili peppers best suited to your liking. It is
wise to sample each chili before using so you will avoid a
pepper that is too hot for your taste.*

Chilies Mild to Wild

The "heat" of chilies is measured by Scoville Units, named after a pharmacologist who established the Scoville Organoleptic Test in 1912. It uses five heat experts who taste and analyze a solution extracted from chili peppers. The "heat" is recorded in multiples of one hundred "Scoville Units." Three of the five analysts must agree before assigning a value to a chili. The Scoville Scale is a subjective measurement, but it is a valuable guide in determining a chili's heat in comparison to other varieties. The Scoville ranking is given for each of the following varieties, with 10 being the hottest.

Anaheim (*chili verde, chili Colorado, New Mexico green or red chili, New Mexico chili, Rio Grande, California pepper, California green chili*)

The anaheim is a popular chili variety, long and narrow, about 6–7 inches long, and light to medium green in color. It is generally mild but can also have a bit of a bite.

In New Mexico, this pepper is called the chili *verde* when green and chili *Colorado* when red. When dried, this is the pepper that makes up those rusty red strings or wreaths of peppers called ristras, a symbol of hope and plenty.

This pepper is the one that is frequently stuffed and used in a host of sauces, particularly in New Mexican cuisine.

HEAT RATING 2: 200–500 Scoville Units

Fresno and Jalapeños These peppers pack a powerful bite. Both varieties are about the same size and rather stocky. (The Fresno is a bit more tapered than the jalapeño.) Fresnos are green or greenish-red, and jalapeños have a deep-green or greenish-black skin. Both varieties turn red as they mature. Both peppers are good for seasoning sauces, minced into dips and salads. Jalapeños have also acquired fame as the crowning touch for nachos.

FRESNO HEAT RATING 5: 2,500–5,000 Scoville Units
JALAPEÑO HEAT RATING 8: 10,000–15,000 Scoville Units

Habañero If you like it hot, the habañero is for you! This chili is about 100 times hotter than a jalapeño or serraño chili. Habañeros change from green to yellow-orange as they ripen. In fresh form they are on the market from September to December and can be found in dried form year round.

Habañeros are used in a number of hot sauces and pickles in the West Indies. Use them sparingly minced or puréed into sauces or wherever you want a special splash of fiery heat. Always wear gloves when handling these peppers. Avoid contact with skin and eyes. When washing hands, use rubbing alcohol to remove the oils; soap and water are not enough for this chili!

HEAT RATING 10: 20,000–80,000 Scoville Units

Poblano As if there isn't enough confusion with chili peppers, sometimes they're marketed under different names, often incorrectly. Such is the case with the poblano, which actually refers to several similar cultivars which are used green. This pepper is sometimes marketed as the Ancho or Pasilla, which are actually different chili varieties altogether.

This glossy, deep-green chili is heart-shaped and generally mild in flavor. These peppers should be roasted and peeled to enhance tenderness and taste. The poblano's thick flesh is ideal for stuffing.

HEAT RATING 4: 1,000–2,500 Scoville Units

Yellow Chili Peppers (*Hungarian wax, banana pepper, sweet banana, hot Hungarian wax, Santa Fe grande, caribe, goldspike, caloro*)

Some yellow peppers are long, tapering, and narrow, while others may be chubby. Their yellow color sometimes turns reddish-orange as they mature.

The heat of these chilies varies widely and at different stages of ripeness. For instance, the banana pepper can be extremely mild, about a heat rating of 3, but when fully mature and red the heat rating soars to nearly an 8!

Sample cautiously and use accordingly. They can be used for pickling, sauces and relishes, garnishing salads, or adding to cornmeal breads or muffins.

HEAT RATING RANGES WIDELY DUE TO VARIETAL DIFFERENCES

Serraño The serraño is very hot with a lasting intensity. It measures about 2-inches long and only ½ inch in diameter, is medium green, and slightly pointed. Because they are small, serraños are not peeled. This variety is popular in Mexico where it is used in guacamole, salsas, and sauces.

HEAT RATING 8: 10,000–15,000 Scoville Units

AVAILABILITY: Year round.

SELECTION AND STORAGE: Select fresh-looking peppers. Store chili peppers in a paper bag in the refrigerator for a week or more.

PREPARATION: Handle chili peppers with care and wear gloves while preparing them because they can burn the skin. After preparation, wash the cutting board with salt and cold water. With extra hot chili peppers, such as the habañero, use rubbing alcohol to remove the oils.

Roasting and peeling chili peppers: Roasting and peeling enhances the texture, develops flavor and succulence, and tempers the heat of most green chilies. There are many ways of roasting. A small quantity can be blistered directly in the flame of a gas range. They should be turned until the skin is blackened all over, about a minute or more.

For a larger quantity, wash the peppers and slit the skin near the stem end. Place chilies on a baking sheet and broil four inches from the heat about 4–6 minutes, turning until they are blistered, but not thoroughly blackened. Remove chili peppers from the heat and wrap in a damp paper towel for about 10 minutes. Pull the skin from the stem to the tip. Scrape away the seeds and membrane with a sharp knife.

A "Hot Tip": The heat in chili peppers is concentrated in the ribs, not in the seeds as many believe, although the seeds can also contain some heat. Therefore, be sure to remove these capsaicin "hot spots" during preparation. Too hot to handle? Cool down the fire with milk or ice cream. Capsaicin, which gives chili peppers their heat, dissolves in fat. So drink milk, rather than water, soda, wine, or beer. Sugar also helps to counteract the heat, so put a little table sugar on your tongue or reach for a hard candy.

NUTRITION INFORMATION: A ¼-cup serving provides vitamin C, is free of sodium, and is just 15 calories.

FIESTA QUESADILLAS

4 anaheim or poblano
  chili peppers
2 scallions
2 cups shredded
  Monterey Jack or
  Cheddar cheese
1 or 2 tablespoons vegetable
  oil, divided

8 flour tortillas, (about 8
  inches in diameter)
  Shredded lettuce
  Chopped tomato
  Guacamole or sour cream

Cut small vertical slits in chili peppers and place on a baking sheet. Broil 4 inches from heat until blistered on all sides, turning every few minutes. Remove from oven, wrap in damp paper towels for a few minutes, then peel off the skin. Scrape away seeds and membrane.

Chop chilies and thinly slice scallions; combine in a medium bowl with the cheese.

In a griddle or skillet, heat 1 tablespoon oil. Sprinkle about 1/3 cup of the cheese mixture over half of each of the tortillas. Fold each tortilla in half. Place tortillas on griddle or skillet, cooking until the cheese melts and the tortillas are crisp on both sides, adding more oil during cooking, if needed. Serve hot, garnished with shredded lettuce, chopped tomato, guacamole, or sour cream.

MAKES 8 QUESADILLAS

CHILIES RELLENOS

8 anaheim chili peppers
3 scallions, thinly sliced
6 ounces Monterey Jack or
  Cheddar cheese,
  shredded (about 1 1/2
  cups)
4 eggs, separated
1/4 cup all-purpose flour

1/2 teaspoon salt
Vegetable oil
Flour
Cilantro sprigs (for
garnish)
Diced tomato (for
garnish)

Pierce each chili at the stem end and place on a baking sheet. Roast the chilies under a broiler, cooking just until the skin is blistered and lightly browned on all sides. Remove from oven. Cover chilies with a damp paper towel. When cool enough to handle, peel off skin. Slice each pepper open lengthwise at the top and remove seeds and membrane. Rinse and pat dry. (You can keep stems on or cut them off, if desired.) Set chilies on paper towels.

In a mixing bowl, toss to combine the scallions and cheese. Spoon about 2–3 tablespoons cheese mixture into each chili (depending on size of pepper), pressing the cut edges in towards the center. (Peppers can be covered with plastic at this point and refrigerated for cooking later.)

In a medium bowl, beat the egg yolks; beat in flour and salt. In a separate bowl, beat egg whites until soft peaks form; fold beaten egg whites into egg yolk mixture.

Heat about 1 inch oil in a large skillet over medium-high heat. Dredge each chili in flour, then dip into the batter, covering it completely; carefully place it into the skillet.

Repeat the process for about half the chilies. Cook them until the underside is lightly browned; turn once and cook the other side. Repeat for the remaining chilies. Drain on paper towels. Serve immediately, garnished with cilantro and diced tomato, if desired.

MAKES 4 SERVINGS

PICADILLO

Picadillo is a familiar dish in every Spanish-speaking country in the Western Hemisphere with many different versions. It deliciously blends the heat of chili peppers, with a combination of vegetables, raisins, olives, and meat all spiced with cinnamon and cloves. Spicy-sweet picadillo is particularly good ladled over sweet potatoes as a main dish or served alongside them.

3 hot chili peppers
(jalapeño or Fresno)
1 medium onion
2 garlic cloves
1 bell pepper
1¹/₂ pounds lean pork or
beef
3 tablespoons vegetable
oil, divided
4 medium tomatoes
¹/₃ cup raisins
6 stuffed olives, thinly
sliced

1 tablespoon red wine
vinegar
¹/₂ teaspoon salt
¹/₄ teaspoon ground
cinnamon
¹/₈ teaspoon ground cloves
Coarsely ground black
pepper
4 large baked or
microwaved sweetpotatoes
(optional)

Remove seeds and membrane from chilies; chop chilies. Peel and chop onion. Peel and mince garlic. Remove seeds and membrane from bell pepper; mince bell pepper. Set vegetables aside.

Trim fat from pork or beef. Cut meat into ¹/₂-inch cubes. Heat 1¹/₂ tablespoons oil in a 3-quart saucepan over medium-high heat. Add meat and cook until it changes color. Add the chilies, onion, garlic, and bell pepper; sauté for 5 minutes or until the vegetables are tender. Meanwhile, peel, seed, and chop tomatoes; set aside.

Drain the liquid from the saucepan. Heat the remaining 1¹/₂ tablespoons oil. Add the tomatoes, raisins, olives, vinegar, salt, and spices; season with black pepper to taste. Cover and cook over low heat 30–40 minutes or until the meat is tender. Serve hot with sweet potatoes as an accompaniment or ladle picadillo over baked or microwaved sweetpotatoes for a main course.

MAKES 4 SERVINGS

GREEN CHILI SAUCE

*A great topping spooned over quesadillas, chicken
enchiladas, or grilled poultry.*

3 anaheim or poblano chili
  peppers
1 cup chicken stock or broth
2 garlic cloves, minced

1 tablespoon cornstarch
1/4 cup chopped cilantro
1/2 cup dairy sour cream or
  plain yogurt

Pierce chili peppers with a knife and place on a baking sheet.
Broil peppers 4 inches from heat until blistered on all sides,
turning every few minutes. Remove from oven, wrap in damp
paper towels for a few minutes, then peel off the skin. Scrape away
seeds and membrane; chop chili peppers.

In a medium saucepan, add the chilies, chicken stock, and
garlic. Bring mixture to a boil, reduce heat, and simmer 20
minutes. In a small cup, add the cornstarch and stir a little of the
hot mixture into it; stir until smooth, then add to chili mixture.
Cook until mixture thickens slightly, then stir in cilantro, sour
cream or yogurt. Cook just enough to heat through.

MAKES 1 CUP

CHINESE CABBAGE

The Orient has provided American cooks with special mild-tasting green vegetables. There are many names for the delicately sweet cabbage varieties of the Brassica species.

Chinese cabbage, or nappa, is more cylindrically-shaped than head cabbage. It has smooth, white ribs and pale green, crinkly leaves prominently striped with white veins.

These varieties have a lighter, more delicate flavor than head cabbage. They're especially well-suited for those who find head cabbage varieties too strong for their appetites. The texture of these cabbages is crunchy, crisp, and juicy, and either variety may be served raw, cooked as greens, stir-fried alone or in combination with other vegetables.

AVAILABILITY: Year round.

SELECTION AND STORAGE: Select fresh-looking leaves with no signs of browning. Store it wrapped in a plastic bag in the refrigerator. Chinese cabbage will keep 1–2 weeks. For use in salads, it's best if used within a few days. A 2-pound Chinese cabbage yields about 8 cups shredded leaves.

PREPARATION: Remove wilted outer leaves from the central core. Wash and use as desired. If serving raw, the leaves can be crisped in ice water. For most cooking purposes, separate the leafy part from the rib since the leaves won't require as much cooking time as the ribs.

To stir-fry: Cut ribs into 2-inch strips and leaves into 2-inch pieces. For 4 to 5 cups of shredded cabbage, heat 1 tablespoon vegetable oil in a large skillet or wok and sauté ribs for 1 minute. Then add 2 tablespoons chicken broth and a little soy sauce, cover, and cook about 3 more minutes, adding the leaves the last 1 to 2 minutes of cooking.

To microwave: For a 1-pound shredded cabbage, place in a 3-quart microwaveable dish. Add 2 tablespoons water, cover, and microwave on high power 4 to 6 minutes, stirring halfway through cooking. Allow to stand a few minutes.

SERVING SUGGESTIONS:

- Serve raw Chinese cabbage shredded or sliced in salads or slaws.
- Use the crisp, raw ribs on crudité platters.
- Combine cabbage ribs and leaves into stir-frys.
- Add to soups or stews.
- Slice into chunks and braise.
- Blanch leaves and use to envelop a favorite stuffing for hors d'oeuvres.

NUTRITION INFORMATION: A 1-cup serving of Chinese cabbage has only 9 calories. It is an excellent source of vitamin C, provides fiber, vitamin A, and potassium, and is very low in sodium.

EGG ROLLS

3/4 pound boneless pork
   Black pepper
2 tablespoons peanut oil
2 teaspoons minced
   gingerroot
2 cups shredded Chinese
   cabbage
1 cup minced celery

1 cup chopped onion
1 1/2 cups fresh bean sprouts
1 tablespoon reduced-
   sodium soy sauce
8 to 10 egg roll wrappers
   Oil for frying
   Sweet-and-Sour Sauce
   (recipe follows)

Trim fat from pork. Mince the pork and season with pepper. In a large skillet, heat the oil and add the pork and gingerroot. Cook until the meat is well-browned. Add the cabbage, celery, and onion to the skillet; sauté for about 2 minutes. Add the bean sprouts and soy sauce and sauté for 1 minute.

With one corner of the egg roll wrapper facing you, place about 3 tablespoons of the filling in the center, spreading mixture to within 1 inch of the left and right corners. Fold the lower corner over the mixture. Fold in the left and right corners, moistening the edges with water. Roll up the wrapper and moisten the edges, pressing to seal.

Pour enough oil into a large skillet to reach a depth of 1/2 inch. Heat the oil. Add the egg rolls and cook over medium-high heat, turning occasionally, until golden brown and crisp on all sides. Cooking will take about 5 minutes. Drain the egg rolls on paper towels. Serve hot with Sweet-and-Sour Sauce I.

MAKES 8 TO 10 EGG ROLLS

SWEET-AND-SOUR SAUCE I

2/3 cup pineapple juice
1/2 cup chicken stock or
   broth
1/4 cup brown sugar
1/4 cup white vinegar

4 teaspoons cornstarch
1 tablespoon reduced-sodium
   soy sauce

In a small saucepan, combine all the ingredients and mix well.
Cook the mixture over medium heat, stirring frequently, until thickened. The sauce will continue to thicken at room temperature.

MAKES 1 1/2 CUPS

CILANTRO

*The lacy and aromatic green-leaved cilantro sprigs are
staples to Asian and Latin cooks. Cilantro, also known as
Chinese Parsley, Mexican Parsley, coriander, and cu-
lantro, has a long history with roots back to the Mediterranean and ancient Egypt. It has recently come to the
attention of American palates with the popularity of Mexi-*

can cuisine. Throughout South and Central America and Asia it is used liberally as well.

The dried seeds of cilantro are marketed as coriander seeds which are used in pickling or ground and combined with other spices for curry powder. These seeds are not interchangeable with fresh coriander in recipes.

AVAILABILITY: Year round.

SELECTION AND STORAGE: Buy fresh-looking bunches, preferably with small stems. Those with roots still attached will keep longer. If the roots are still attached, place the stems in a small container of water, cover with a plastic bag, and refrigerate. It should keep 1–2 weeks when stored this way. If cilantro is purchased without the roots, wrap the stems in damp paper towels, enclose in plastic, refrigerate, and use within a few days.

PREPARATION: Wash cilantro right before use, then blot dry and use immediately.

SERVING SUGGESTIONS:

- Cilantro combines well with tomatillos, chili peppers, and tomatoes.
- Use in salsas.
- Flavor soups, stews, and sauces with the roots as well as the stems and leaves.
- Feature cilantro's lacy leaves as a garnish.

NUTRITION INFORMATION: A 1-cup serving contains vitamin A and just 5 calories.

SALSA FRESCA

*There are many variations of salsas that can be used as a
dip for chips or as a topping for grilled poultry or
seafood. Salsa can serve as an accompaniment to Southwestern specialties.*

3 large tomatoes
1 small onion
2 garlic cloves
⅓ cup chopped fresh
   cilantro
3 tablespoons fresh lime
   juice

3–4 tablespoons minced
   jalapeño or hot chili*
Salt and coarsely
   ground black pepper

Dice tomatoes. Peel and chop onion. Peel and mince garlic.
Combine all ingredients in a bowl, season with salt and pepper to
taste. Allow to stand at room temperature for 1 hour to blend
flavors. Salsa can be kept up to 2 days if covered and refrigerated.

MAKES ABOUT 3 CUPS

* Adjust amount of chili depending on your taste preference.

CHICKEN SALSA SALAD

1½ pounds boneless chicken
   breasts
4 teaspoons ground cumin
1½ teaspoons garlic powder
½ teaspoon salt
¼ teaspoon ground
   cayenne pepper
¼ cup plus 1½
   tablespoons corn oil,
   divided
   Grated peel from 1
   orange

3 tablespoons freshly
   squeezed orange juice
⅓ cup cider vinegar
1 cup peeled and julienne-
   cut jícama
1 cup diced red onion
⅓ cup minced fresh cilantro
1 tablespoon minced
   jalapeño pepper
2 large tomatoes, seeded
   and chopped
   Shredded lettuce
   Cilantro sprigs

Remove any skin from chicken; cut into 1-inch cubes. In a bowl, combine cumin, garlic powder, salt, and cayenne; mix well. Toss the chicken in the cumin mixture. In a medium nonstick skillet, heat 1½ tablespoons oil; add chicken and cook over medium-high heat 4–6 minutes or until done. Remove chicken from skillet and place in a 2-quart bowl.

In a cup, combine grated orange peel and juice, vinegar, and remaining ¼ cup oil; mix well. Pour mixture over chicken and cool about 15 minutes. Meanwhile, prepare jícama, onion, cilantro, and jalapeño. When chicken has cooled, add jícama, onion, cilantro, and jalapeño to the bowl; gently toss to coat with the mixture. Cover and chill at least 30 minutes.

At serving time, add tomato to chicken mixture and gently toss. Divide lettuce on 4 individual dinner plates or on a serving platter. Mound chicken mixture over the lettuce and garnish with cilantro sprigs.

MAKES 4 SERVINGS

CILANTRO PESTO

A great sauce for pasta.

1 cup cilantro leaves
and stems (about 2
ounces)
2 or 3 garlic cloves
$^1/_2$ cup pine nuts
$^1/_3$ cup olive oil

$^1/_2$ cup grated Parmesan
cheese or a mixture of
grated Romano and
Parmesan cheese
$^1/_4$ teaspoon salt
Coarsely ground black
pepper

Trim any roots from cilantro. Wash cilantro well and pat dry. Pack tightly into 1 cup measure. Peel garlic.

To make pesto with a food processor: Combine cilantro, garlic, pine nuts, and salt; process just until cilantro is finely minced. With the motor running, gradually add the oil through the feed tube. Stir in cheese and season with pepper to taste.

To make pesto with a blender: Place cilantro, garlic, pine nuts, salt, and oil in the blender; cover and process until mixture is a thick purée. Stir in cheese and season with pepper to taste.

MAKES 1 CUP (ENOUGH FOR 1 POUND OF PASTA)

$\mathcal{D}$AIKON

Often resembling a large, white carrot, this Oriental radish is mild, sweet, and juicy. A member of the crucifer or mustard family, and close relative of the cherry red radish, it has familiar peppery flavor.

This Oriental staple varies in size and shape—those found in the supermarket range from $1/2$ to about 2 pounds. The daikon sold in Oriental markets can be much larger and its color can be greenish, rose, black, or other variations. These flavorful roots are sometimes sold with their peppery green tops attached.

Daikon contains the enzyme diastase, which aids in the digestion of starches. As rice lovers, the Japanese use the crunchy root daily and have hundreds of ways to prepare it. A traditional preparation is to grate it and serve as an accompaniment to raw fish dishes. In Japan, pickled daikon called, takuan, is as popular as American pickled cucumbers.

AVAILABILITY: Year round, but fall and winter crops are mild while spring and summer crops tend to be spicy.

SELECTION AND STORAGE: Look for firm, smooth radishes

with a pearly sheen. Contrary to their hardy appearance, Oriental radishes are not durable and will quickly lose their flavor. Keep daikon wrapped in plastic and refrigerated. They are best if used within a few days.

PREPARATION: The skin is thin so peeling is a matter of preference. Scrubbing is all that is needed.

SERVING SUGGESTIONS:

- Stir-fry slices or julienne strips alone or in combination with other vegetables.
- Flavor soups and stews with daikon.
- Serve slices as crunchy "chips" for dips.
- Toss shredded, sliced, or julienned daikon into salads.
- Daikon's firm and sturdy texture is perfect for carving flowers and other interesting shapes suitable for garnishing.

NUTRITION INFORMATION: A 2-ounce serving provides vitamin C, fiber, and other nutrients, and has about 10 calories.

JULIENNE OF DAIKON AND RED PEPPER WITH SZECHWAN-STYLE DRESSING

1/2 pound daikon
1 medium, red bell pepper

4 scallions
Szechwan-Style Dressing

SZECHWAN-STYLE DRESSING

2 tablespoons rice vinegar or
  white wine vinegar
2 teaspoons sugar
2 teaspoons reduced-sodium
  soy sauce

2 teaspoons sesame oil
3/4 teaspoon hot pepper sauce
2 tablespoons peanut oil

Scrub or peel daikon; cut into 2-inch long julienne strips. Remove seeds and membrane from red pepper; cut into thin strips about 2-inches long. Thinly slice scallions. Combine the vegetables in a medium bowl. In a liquid measure, combine all the Szechwan-Style Dressing ingredients; mix well. Pour dressing over vegetables. Chill until serving time.

MAKES 4 SERVINGS

CURRIED RICE AND VEGETABLE SALAD

2 cups long-grain white rice
1 daikon, about 8 ounces
1 medium carrot
1 medium, red bell pepper
6 scallions

Curry Dressing (recipe
  follows)
1/2 cup chopped salted
  peanuts or toasted
  almonds

Cook rice according to package directions until tender. Transfer to a large bowl.

Peel and thinly slice the daikon and carrot. Remove the seeds and membrane from the pepper, cut pepper into thin slices, about 2-inches long. Thinly slice the scallions.

Add all the vegetables to the same bowl as the rice. Pour the

Curry Dressing over the mixture and toss to coat. Cover and chill for at least 1 hour. Right before serving, stir in the chopped peanuts or toasted almonds.

MAKES 6 TO 8 SERVINGS

CURRY DRESSING

1 cup plain yogurt
1 tablespoon curry powder
2 tablespoons chutney

1 tablespoon fresh lemon juice
1 tablespoon Dijon mustard

In a medium bowl, combine all the dressing ingredients. Stir until well-blended.

MAKES ABOUT 1 CUP

*E*GGPLANT

The "apple of love," a romantic name for eggplant, has indeed been adored in many countries since antiquity. Eggplant was cultivated in both India and China, brought to Europe via the Middle East along the silk route, and then on to America.

Eggplant was named for the small, white, egg-shaped varieties that were introduced to the English during the seventeenth century. The name is now firmly rooted even for the purple-skinned variety with which we are familiar.

Today there is a bevy of eggplant varieties, available in a range of colors, shapes, and sizes. Most eggplants are similar enough to be interchangeable, but some variations in texture and flavor exist.

Here are brief characteristics of some varieties you may encounter:

- Casper: White-skinned, slender, about 6 inches long.
- Chinese White: White-skinned, slender, somewhat banana-shaped with a curved end.
- Easter Egg: White-skinned, round, about the size of a tennis ball or smaller; somewhat bitter.
- French: Shaped like the Easter Egg variety with a deep purple skin.
- Italian: Resembling an ordinary eggplant but in miniature with a delicate skin and smooth flesh. The Rosa Bianca is a purplish-lavender streaked with white.
- Japanese: A small, slender version of the American eggplant, generally about 5–7 inches long. These eggplants have a slightly sweet, mild flavor.
- Puerto Rican/Rayada: About 4–6 inches long with a purple and white streaked skin.
- Thai: Sold mainly in Asian markets, these can be purple, white, green, or green-streaked. The tiny, green Thai eggplant is bunched like grapes and crunchy in texture; other Thai varieties can be as large as an orange with a more traditional eggplant texture.

AVAILABILITY: Year round.

SELECTION AND STORAGE: Choose eggplants that are firm and heavy for their size. Avoid any flabby, bronzed, or pitted specimens, indicating age and a tendency toward bitterness. Keep refrigerated in plastic and use within a few days.

PREPARATION: Slice off the cap and peel the skin, if desired. Procedures for many eggplant recipes often suggest salting slices 20–30 minutes prior to cooking, a method some cooking experts believe help to extract any existing bitterness. Salting is not a necessary step, but it does help to remove excess moisture which keeps it from exuding juices while cooking. Salting also reduces the amount of oil needed for cooking, a benefit for health-conscious consumers.

If you choose to salt, place cut, salted eggplant in a colander, weighted down for about 20–30 minutes, pressing out the moisture with paper towels, then prepare as desired.

SERVING SUGGESTIONS:

- Eggplant is versatile and adapts well to many preparation methods such as baking, sautéing, broiling, and grilling.
- Its subtle flavor is well-complemented with ingredients such as garlic, onions, tomatoes, herbs, and cheese.
- Stuff halves with vegetables, meats, or cheeses.
- Dip slices into egg white then dredge in a mixture of seasoned bread crumbs and Parmesan cheese and fry until golden brown.

NUTRITION INFORMATION: A $1/2$-cup serving of cooked, steamed eggplant is free of sodium, provides folacin (a B-vitamin) and dietary fiber, and has about 13 calories.

EGGPLANT-OLIVE APPETIZER SPREAD

*This is a version of a popular Middle Eastern appetizer,
Baba Ghanoush, served with toasted pita bread. The
tahini, or sesame paste, is a traditional ingredient, but the
spread is equally good without it.*

1 1/2 pounds eggplant
3 tablespoons fresh lemon
  juice
2 tablespoons tahini
  (optional)
1 tablespoon olive oil
1 garlic clove, minced
1/2 teaspoon salt

1/2 cup chopped pimento-
  stuffed olives*
2 tablespoons minced fresh
  parsley
1/4 cup toasted pine nuts
  (optional)
  Toasted pita bread
  triangles

Pierce eggplant with a fork in several places. Preheat oven to
400° F. Place eggplant on baking sheet and bake for 25 minutes.
Turn on the broiler, then place eggplant under the heat, rotating
until the skin is blistered all over and eggplant is tender. Remove
from oven. When cool enough to handle, peel the eggplant and
squeeze out the juice.

In a blender or food processor, combine eggplant, lemon juice,
tahini, olive oil, garlic, and salt; purée until smooth. Stir in the
olives. Transfer to a serving dish and cool. Garnish with parsley
and pine nuts, if desired. Serve with toasted pita triangles.

MAKES ABOUT 2 CUPS

* For variation, substitute chopped black olives for half the pimento-stuffed olives.

EGGPLANT-TOMATO STACKS

1 pound eggplant
Olive oil
Salt
2 medium tomatoes
1 1/2 tablespoons minced
   fresh basil

Freshly ground black
   pepper
4 ounces (1 cup shredded)
   mozzarella cheese

Peel eggplant, if desired; cut crosswise into 1/2-inch thick slices. Place slices on a lightly oiled baking sheet. Brush eggplant with olive oil; sprinkle with salt. Place about 4 inches under broiler; broil 4–5 minutes or until lightly browned. Turn eggplant over, baste with more oil and season with salt. Continue cooking 4–5 minutes more or until browned. Remove from broiler. Place one tomato slice on top of each slice of eggplant. Sprinkle with basil and season with pepper; top with cheese. Return to broiler and broil just until cheese melts.

MAKES 4 SERVINGS

JAPANESE EGGPLANT WITH SPICY SESAME SAUCE

1 1/2 pounds Japanese
   eggplant
2 tablespoons sesame oil
1 tablespoon tahini
   (sesame paste)
1 tablespoon reduced-
   sodium soy sauce
2 teaspoons sugar

1 teaspoon rice vinegar or
   cider vinegar
1 teaspoon chili oil
1 garlic clove
1/2 teaspoon minced fresh
   ginger
2 scallions

Preheat oven to 400° F. Lightly coat the bottom of a baking pan
with oil or a nonstick cooking spray. Prick eggplants with a fork
and bake for 20 minutes. Then set under the broiler a few minutes
rotating eggplants until the skin is blistered. Remove from broiler.
When cool enough to handle, rub the charred skin off.

In a cup, combine remaining ingredients. Cut eggplants lengthwise into halves. Serve halves warm or chilled; drizzle with the
sauce right before serving.

MAKES 4 SERVINGS

VEGETABLE MÉLANGE IN PUFF PASTRY

1 eggplant, about 1
  pound
  Salt
1 medium onion
2 garlic cloves
2 medium carrots
1¹/2 cups chopped, fresh
  broccoli florets
5 tablespoons vegetable or
  olive oil, divided
¹/2 teaspoon salt

1 tablespoon minced fresh
  oregano or 1 teaspoon
  dried oregano
  Coarsely ground black
  pepper
1 sheet frozen puff pastry,
  thawed
1 cup shredded mozzarella
  cheese
1 egg white
2 teaspoons water

Peel and finely dice eggplant (you should have about 4 cups).
Sprinkle eggplant with salt; allow to drain for 20–30 minutes; pat
dry. Meanwhile, peel and chop onion; peel and mince garlic. Peel
and shred carrots; chop broccoli florets into very small pieces; set
aside.

In a large skillet, heat 3 tablespoons oil. Add eggplant, onion, and garlic; sauté over medium heat 4–5 minutes. Add remaining 2 tablespoons oil. Stir in carrots and broccoli; stir-fry an additional 3 minutes. Remove from heat; add salt and oregano. Season with pepper to taste.

Preheat oven to 400° F. Roll out pastry to a 14-inch square. Place pastry on a large, ungreased baking sheet. Spread vegetable mixture over half the pastry, leaving a ¹/₂-inch border around the edges. Sprinkle cheese over the vegetables. Fold pastry over the vegetables. Press edges of the pastry together to seal then press edges up along the pastry.

In a small bowl, beat the egg white with the water. Brush just enough of the egg mixture over the pastry to cover it. Bake for 18–20 minutes or until the pastry is golden brown and puffed. Allow to stand about 5 minutes before cutting. Cut crosswise into slices and serve immediately.

MAKES 4 MAIN-COURSE SERVINGS

IMAM BAYILDI

This is an adaptation of a traditional Turkish recipe which translates as the "swooning Imam." According to the Middle Eastern story, whenever the religious leader's wives served this dish, he swooned in ecstasy. That is certainly a provocative tale for such a worldly vegetable!

4 Japanese eggplants, each
   about 6–8 ounces
   Salt
1 medium onion
3 garlic cloves
2 large tomatoes
   About ¹/₃ cup olive oil,
   divided

1 tablespoon chopped fresh
   oregano or 1 teaspoon
   dried oregano
¹/₄ teaspoon salt
   Freshly ground black
   pepper
2 tablespoons minced fresh
   parsley

Wash eggplants and slice off stems. Cut eggplants into halves lengthwise. On each half, skin side up, make a lengthwise V-shaped incision, about 1-inch wide and 1/2-inch deep, running the length of the eggplant. Sprinkle all cut sides with salt. Place halves on paper towels weighted on the top; set aside.

Meanwhile, peel and slice onion crosswise into 1/8-inch rings. Peel and mince garlic. Peel, seed, and chop tomatoes. In a large, nonstick skillet, heat 1 1/2 tablespoons oil. Add onion and sauté over medium heat about 5 minutes or until onion is tender. Add garlic and tomatoes, sauté 5–8 minutes longer. Add oregano, salt, and season with pepper; set aside.

Squeeze out moisture from eggplant and pat with a paper towel. In a large, nonstick skillet, heat 3 tablespoons oil. Arrange eggplants flat sides down, and cook over medium heat until lightly browned, adding more oil, if needed. Turn eggplants and cook about 5 minutes more. Then stuff the hollowed eggplant strips with the tomato-onion mixture. Cover, reduce to simmer, and cook 8–10 minutes or until tender, adding more oil to the skillet, if needed during cooking. Sprinkle with parsley and serve hot or refrigerate and serve cold.

MAKES 4 SERVINGS

EGGPLANT PARMESAN

2 pounds eggplant
Salt
2 garlic cloves
1 medium onion
3 medium tomatoes
2 tablespoons olive oil
6 ounces tomato paste
1/4 cup water
1 teaspoon dried basil,
   divided

1 teaspoon dried oregano,
   divided
1/4 teaspoon salt
2 eggs or 3 egg whites
1 cup dry bread crumbs
3/4 cup Parmesan cheese,
   divided
Oil for frying
8 ounces mozzarella
   cheese, shredded

Peel eggplant and slice into 1/4-inch slices. Sprinkle with salt and set aside while preparing sauce.

Peel and mince garlic. Peel and chop onion. Peel, seed, and chop tomatoes. Heat olive oil in a saucepan. Add garlic and onion; sauté about 4–5 minutes or until soft. Stir in tomatoes, tomato paste, water, 1/2 teaspoon each of the herbs, and the salt. Simmer sauce while preparing eggplant.

Pat eggplant slices with a paper towel. In a small bowl, beat eggs or egg whites with 2 teaspoons water. In another bowl, combine bread crumbs, 1/2 cup Parmesan cheese, and a 1/2 teaspoon each of basil and oregano; toss to mix. Dip eggplant slices into eggs, then coat with the crumb mixture.

Heat about 1/4 cup oil in a large, nonstick skillet; sauté eggplant until golden brown on both sides. Remove and drain on paper towels. Continue cooking slices, adding more oil as needed.

Spoon about one-third of the tomato sauce in the bottom of a lightly oiled 8-inch-square baking pan. Place eggplant slices to cover the bottom. Sprinkle with about one-third the mozzarella and 2 tablespoons Parmesan cheese. Repeat the layers, ending with the cheeses. Bake in preheated 350° F oven for about 20 minutes or until bubbly.

MAKES ABOUT 6 SERVINGS

*F*EIJOA

Also known as the pineapple guava, the round or egg-shaped feijoa (pronounced fay-JO-ah) is a sub-tropical fruit native to Brazil. It is not a guava, although it is a member of the same botanical family, the Myrtaceae or myrtle family.

The feijoa's taste and aroma are elusive with hints of pineapple, lemon, passion fruit, and guava. They are tangy and fragrant.

Feijoas are about 2¹/₂–3 inches long, with a waxy, olive green to grayish-green skin. Its pale yellow or cream-colored flesh is slightly granular like some pear varieties. Tiny edible seeds are embedded in its jellylike center.

AVAILABILITY: Crops from New Zealand from late winter through early June and from California from September through December.

SELECTION AND STORAGE: Feijoas are tree-ripened, but some may require a day or two at room temperature to soften slightly. They should yield a bit to palm pressure. Store ripe fruit in the refrigerator and use within a day or two.

PREPARATION: To scoop out of the shell, simply cut into halves, sprinkle with sugar, if desired, and scoop fruit with a spoon. For other uses, peel the fruit with a sharp knife, and cut crosswise into slices. Once cut, the flesh darkens, so coat cut surfaces with lemon, lime, or orange juice to preserve their color.

SERVING SUGGESTIONS:

- Add slices to fruit salads.
- Poach in a sugar syrup and serve chilled or combine with other fruits, particularly with other tropical fruits.
- Purée and use for fruit smoothies or a fruit sauce.
- Drizzle slices with orange-flavored liqueur and serve with vanilla ice cream, yogurt, or lemon sherbet.
- The feijoa's high pectin content is perfect for jams and jellies.

NUTRITION INFORMATION: A good source of vitamin C, and a 3½-ounce serving has about 35 calories.

FEIJOAS A L'ORANGE

Poached and chilled slices of feijoa topped with a dollop of whipped cream and tiny, tangy-sweet slivers of orange peel for a light dessert, or add the slices to fruit compotes.

Peel from ½ orange
6 feijoas
⅓ cup water
⅓ cup plus 2 teaspoons sugar, divided

⅓ cup heavy cream
½ cup fresh raspberries or sliced strawberries

Cut orange peel into very thin strips, removing any white membrane from strips. In a small saucepan, bring 1 cup water to a boil. Add orange strips; cover and cook over medium heat for 5 minutes. Drain and reserve.

Meanwhile, peel and cut feijoas crosswise into 1/4-inch thick slices; set aside. In a large skillet, combine orange peel, 1/3 cup water, and 1/3 cup sugar. Bring mixture to a boil; boil 3 minutes. Reduce heat to low; add sliced feijoas, cover, and cook 2 minutes more. Remove from heat. Spoon into a dish, cover, and chill.

At serving time, whip the cream until soft peaks form. Beat in the 2 teaspoons sugar. To serve, arrange the slices in a circle on 4 dessert plates. Place some of the orange slivers and a few berries on each plate. Drizzle a little of the syrup over the berries. Top with a dollop of whipped cream and garnish with a few orange slivers.

MAKES 4 SERVINGS

MINTED FEIJOA AND MELON

3 tablespoons sugar
1/4 cup water
2 tablespoons chopped
   fresh mint
1 tablespoon fresh orange
   juice
2 teaspoons fresh lemon or
   lime juice

4 feijoas
1 cup cantaloupe or
   Crenshaw melon balls
1 cup watermelon balls
Mint sprigs

In a small saucepan, combine sugar and water. Bring mixture to a boil; boil 2 minutes. Remove from heat; stir in mint. Chill 30 minutes; strain through a fine-meshed sieve into a 1 1/2-quart bowl; discard mint. Stir in juices.

Peel and slice feijoas crosswise into ¼-inch slices; place them in the bowl with the mint mixture. Cover and chill for 30 minutes; add melon balls and toss gently to coat with the mint mixture. Serve or cover and refrigerate for up to 2 hours. Garnish with mint sprigs.

MAKES 4 SERVINGS

FRESH FRUITS IN GRAND MARNIER

4 feijoas
2 mangos
2 purple or red-skinned plums
2 cups halved fresh
    strawberries
1 cup red grapes

¼ cup Grand Marnier or
    other orange liqueur
3 tablespoons fresh orange
    juice
1 tablespoon sugar

Peel and slice feijoas crosswise. Peel and pit mango; cut into chunks. Remove pits from plums; cut plums into wedges. Combine all fruits in a medium glass bowl. In a cup, combine Grand Marnier, orange juice, and sugar; pour mixture over fruits. Cover and refrigerate at least ½ hour, tossing occasionally with the juice.

MAKES 6 TO 8 SERVINGS

$\mathcal{F}$ENNEL

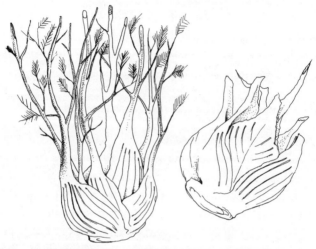

Fennel is a distinctive vegetable both in appearance and taste. Its pale green, celerylike stalks extend from an enlarged base, which is crowned with feathery green fronds. The flavor of fennel is reminiscent of licorice or anise, yet sweeter. As a result of its unique flavor, fennel is sometimes marketed as anise.

Fennel is also marketed by its Italian name, finocchio, illustrating its close connections to Italian cooking. It is native to the Mediterranean and has been a favorite in Italy since ancient times. Romans cultivated fennel to season meats, seafood, and sauces. Traditionally, Italians serve fennel in any part of the meal, from appetizers to dessert. It is commercially cultivated in Italy, France, and Greece as well as in the United States.

Fennel is most prized for its enlarged base, referred to as the "bulb." The base may be either flat and elongated or round and bulbous. The stalks, if still attached, can be simmered in soups and stews for flavoring. Unlike celery, fennel stalks tend to be fibrous and benefit from cooking to soften them.

Served raw, fennel's licorice qualities are more pronounced, and it cleanses the palate with its aromatic crispness. For this reason, this vegetable is well-suited as a dessert course. When cooked, fennel's sweet and distinctive flavor is transformed into something more delicate.

AVAILABILITY: September through May.

SELECTION AND STORAGE: Look for firm, light green or white bulbs with fresh-looking tops (if attached). Avoid any soft bulbs or those with cracked or discolored bases. Allow about half of a 4-inch bulb per serving. If the stalks are still attached, trim them from the bulbs at home, and wrap separately in plastic. Fennel bulbs should be used within a few days, but if in good condition can keep up to one week; the stalks should be used within 3 to 4 days.

PREPARATION: Trim off any wilted or bruised areas. Trim stalks to within 1 inch of the bulb. Reserve both the stalks and leaves. Use the stalks for flavoring soups, stews, and sauces, and use the leaves for a delicate garnish, or chop them and add to tossed or seafood salads.

Remove the core in the base of the bulb, as well as the first layers of the base, which are more fibrous. Older fennel may require stringing like celery—simply insert the tip of a paring knife just under the flesh, then pull the strip toward the base.

If fennel seems to be in need of refreshing, soak it in ice water in the refrigerator for about an hour.

To serve raw, cut fennel vertically into halves and then wedges. It can be cut diagonally for sautéeing. If you're planning to braise or bake fennel, the bulbs can be halved or quartered.

SERVING SUGGESTIONS:

- Use slices in stir-fry combinations.
- Serve braised halved bulbs as an accompaniment to roasts.
- Thinly slice raw fennel, or blanch first, and drizzle with a vinaigrette.
- Add fennel's distinctive flavor to soups or stews.
- Parboil sliced fennel, coat with a batter or dip into beaten egg and dry bread crumbs, then fry in oil until golden.
- Sprinkle braised and halved bulbs with Parmesan cheese, dot with margarine or butter, pour a little chicken broth into a pan, and bake about 30 minutes at 400° F.

NUTRITION INFORMATION: Fennel provides fiber, some vitamin A, and other nutrients. It has just 30 calories per cup. In fact its low-fat, low-calorie attributes have long been known—ancient Greeks called fennel "marathon," from the verb *maraino*, meaning "to grow thin."

FENNEL TEMPURA

Crunchy bite-size pieces of fennel are enveloped in a light, crispy batter.

4 medium fennel bulbs	1/4 teaspoon salt
2 eggs	Vegetable oil
3/4 cup all-purpose flour	Fresh lemon or lime juice
1/3 cup milk	(optional)

Trim stalks from fennel bulbs. Remove cores at base and cut bulbs into bite-size pieces. Place in a vegetable steamer basket and cook over boiling water for 6–8 minutes. Remove from heat and drain on paper towels.

In a medium mixing bowl, beat eggs and stir in flour, milk, and salt. Mix until well-blended and smooth.

Pour oil into a large skillet to a depth of ³/₄ inch. Heat oil to a temperature of about 365° F on a candy/deep fry thermometer. If no thermometer is available, the temperature can be tested by placing a 1-inch cube of bread in the oil when you think it's hot. If the cube browns in 60 seconds, the oil is ready for frying.

Dip fennel into batter and then fry until crisp and golden brown on both sides. Drain on paper towels. Squeeze lemon or lime juice over tempura if desired and serve hot.

MAKES 4 TO 6 SERVINGS

VEGETABLES IN YOGURT

1 medium fennel bulb	¹/₄ cup chopped onion
1 large cucumber	1 cup plain yogurt
2 large carrots	Salt and pepper
1 garlic clove	

Trim fennel and cut the bulb into thin slices. Peel the cucumber and cut into thin slices. Scrape carrots and shred. Peel and mince garlic. In a mixing bowl combine fennel, cucumber, carrots, garlic, and onion. Add yogurt and season with salt and pepper to taste. Toss to coat. Chill before serving.

MAKES 4 SERVINGS

DILLED FENNEL SALAD

3 large fennel bulbs	1 garlic clove, minced
1 small onion	1 tablespoon chopped fresh
1 medium tomato	dill or 1 teaspoon dill
¹/₃ cup vegetable or olive oil	weed
3 tablespoons red wine	¹/₄ teaspoon salt
vinegar	Lettuce leaves

Trim fennel stalks and leaves from the bulbs. Cut bulbs into thin slices. Peel and chop the onion. Chop the tomato. Combine the fennel, onion, and tomato in a medium mixing bowl.

In a screw-top jar, combine the oil, vinegar, garlic, dill, and salt. Shake well to blend. Pour the mixture over the vegetables and gently toss to coat them. Chill the salad for 1 hour. Serve on a bed of lettuce.

MAKES 4 SERVINGS

FENNEL ITALIANO

2 medium fennel bulbs
1 garlic clove
1 small onion
1 pound fresh mushrooms
1 large tomato
2–3 tablespoons olive oil

1 tablespoon chopped fresh basil or 1 teaspoon dried basil
Salt and coarsely ground black pepper

Trim fennel and cut bulbs into 1-inch pieces. Peel and mince garlic. Peel and chop onion. Wipe the mushrooms with a damp cloth, trim stems, and slice mushrooms. Blanch the tomato, peel, seed, and chop.

Heat 2 tablespoons oil in a large skillet. Add the fennel, garlic, and onion. Sauté over medium heat for 2–3 minutes. Add mushrooms and cook for about 3 minutes more, adding more oil if necessary. Then add the chopped tomato, basil, and salt and pepper to taste; sauté until heated through. Serve hot.

MAKES 4 SERVINGS

GINGERROOT

A food gift from the Orient, golden-skinned ginger is a powerhouse of lively flavor. Fresh ginger provides sharp contrast to the more subtle ground spice.

Gingerroot is a popular ingredient in Indian, Thai, Malaysian, and Oriental cookery. It is believed to be a native of tropical southeastern Asia and has been used since antiquity. Gingerroot was carried from Asia into the Mediterranean and Europe and was later introduced into the West Indies and Mexico by the Spaniards. This spicy flavoring ingredient is now commercially produced in Hawaii, Puerto Rico, Fiji, Taiwan, Philippines, Costa Rica, and Brazil.

Gingerroot botanically is a rhizome, not a root. The irregularly-shaped roots, called "hands," vary widely in size. Underneath its golden brown or pinkish tinged skin is a yellow juicy flesh bursting with lively flavor. Gingerroot must be young and tender to be at its finest. The smaller knobs radiating from the main root are more delicate in flavor.

AVAILABILITY: Year round.

SELECTION AND STORAGE: Select fresh-looking, firm roots with shiny skin, avoiding any that are shriveled. Gingerroot can be stored in a cool, dry place up to one month. Once cut, it should be wrapped in plastic and refrigerated. Peeled and sliced ginger can be stored up to a year, if placed in a tightly sealed container, covered with dry sherry, and refrigerated.

PREPARATION: Peel the skin then grate, mince, or slice the yellow flesh according to a recipe's requirements. To substitute fresh ginger for the ground spice, use about 1 tablespoon grated fresh gingerroot for 1/4 teaspoon ground ginger.

SERVING SUGGESTIONS:

- Steep ginger slices in hot water for teas and other beverages.
- Spice up stir-fry recipes with minced gingerroot.
- Combine minced gingerroot in marinades.
- Use for flavoring salad dressings, fruits, vegetables, seafood, poultry, meats, soups, and quick breads.

NUTRITION INFORMATION: Used in such small amounts, its nutrition and calorie contributions are slight. Five thin slices provide some vitamin C and potassium, and contain 8 calories.

GINGER MARINADE

Use this fresh ginger marinade for chicken or turkey.

3 tablespoons reduced-
    sodium soy sauce
1 tablespoon cornstarch
3 tablespoons fresh lemon
    juice

3 tablespoons sesame oil
3 tablespoons minced, fresh
    gingerroot
2 tablespoons honey
1 garlic clove, minced

In a cup, stir together soy sauce and cornstarch until smooth. Add remaining ingredients and stir until well-blended. Pour over chicken or turkey breasts. Allow to marinate at least 1 hour.

MAKES ENOUGH TO MARINATE 2 POUNDS CHICKEN OR TURKEY

SPICED LIMEADE

*1 - inch knob of fresh
    gingerroot*
1 1/2 quarts water
8 whole cloves

4 whole allspice
1 – 1 1/4 cups sugar
8 or 9 limes

Cut the gingerroot into thin slices. In a large saucepan, combine the ginger, water, and spices. Bring the mixture to a boil, then reduce the heat and simmer for 20 minutes. Strain the mixture through a sieve and discard the ginger slices and spices. Add sugar to the liquid and stir until it is dissolved. Squeeze the limes and measure 3/4 cup juice. Add to the syrup; test for sweetness, adding more sugar if desired. Remove from heat and cool. Pour the liquid into a covered container and refrigerate. Serve over ice.

MAKES ABOUT 1 1/2 QUARTS

$\mathcal{H}$ORNED MELON/KIWANO

The African horned melon, also known as the Kiwano or jelly melon, has a thick rind that is golden yellow to orange when ripe and covered with a mass of spiky protrusions. White, cucumberlike seeds are suspended in a lime green, translucent flesh, which is jellylike in texture. Its tart flavor hints of lime and cucumber.

This member of the Cucumis family was originally grown in southwest Africa perhaps for its thirst-quenching qualities. For over 60 years, it has been cultivated in New Zealand and more recently in California. Kiwano is a trademarked brand name by some New Zealand growers who know firsthand what a difference a name makes—once the Chinese gooseberry was renamed the kiwifruit, its sales and popularity soared. Perhaps this will be the fate of yet another green-fleshed fruit!

AVAILABILITY: Year round, with supplies from New Zealand March through mid-July; supplies from California July through December; supplies from storage December through March.

SELECTION AND STORAGE: Select fruit golden yellow or bright orange in color. Store in a cool, dry place. Do not refrigerate. Horned melons are excellent keepers.

PREPARATION: While some promotional literature suggests halving the fruit lengthwise or cutting into wedges and eating right out of the shell, even with a good dose of sweetening, this method doesn't do the fruit justice. Its jellylike flesh is best puréed, strained (if desired, or depending on the recipe), and sweetened for sauces, dressings, beverages, sorbets, and more.

SERVING SUGGESTIONS:

- Halve fruit; scoop out pulp and seeds; reserving shells. Purée mixture, flavor with a little lime juice and sweeten to taste; strain mixture. Scoop seasonal fresh fruit in melon halves and drizzle with the puréed melon.
- Spoon strained and sweetened pulp over frozen yogurt or ice cream.
- Use fruit purée in cocktails, punches, and other beverages.
- Feature its lime green color as an interesting fruit sauce.

NUTRITION INFORMATION: A 3$^1/_2$-ounce serving is a good source of vitamins A and C, provides fiber, and has 24 calories.

KIWANO COCKTAIL

1 kiwano	*$^1/_2$ cup rum*
2 tablespoons orange liqueur	*Carambola or lime slices (for garnish)*
$^1/_3$ cup superfine sugar	
1 tablespoon fresh lime juice	

Halve kiwano lengthwise; scoop out pulp and seeds. Place in a blender; whirl until puréed. Strain. Combine strained mixture and remaining ingredients. Chill thoroughly. Serve over crushed ice in highball glasses, garnished with carambola or lime.

MAKES 1 CUP (ABOUT 4 DRINKS)

TROPICAL AMBROSIA

*The mint green kiwano dressing is a refreshing
complement to tropical fresh fruit.*

1 kiwano	*¹/₂ fresh pineapple*
1 cup vanilla yogurt	*Lettuce leaves*
1 cup fresh strawberries	*Toasted shredded coconut*
1 papaya	

To prepare sauce, halve Kiwano lengthwise. Scoop out pulp and seeds. In a blender or food processor process pulp and seeds to a purée. Strain out seeds. Combine strained mixture and yogurt. Chill.

Halve berries. Peel papaya and cut lengthwise into ¹/₄-inch slices. Peel and core pineapple. Cut into spears. Arrange fruits on lettuce leaves. Spoon sauce over fruit and sprinkle with coconut.

MAKES 4 SERVINGS

*J*ERUSALEM ARTICHOKES

The Jerusalem artichoke has suffered a long-standing identity crisis. The knobby, potatolike tubers are neither botanically related to the globe artichoke (although its flavor is vaguely reminiscent when cooked), nor are they from Jerusalem. In fact, they are native to American soil.

During the early-seventeenth century, French explorer Samuel Champlain found the Indians on Cape Cod growing the tuber. He took it back to Europe as a novelty where it was quickly cultivated and made popular. Italians called the plant with the yellow blossom girasole, meaning "turning to the sun" (the plant is in fact a member of the sunflower genus, Helianthus tuberosus). However, the English may have mispronounced the name and it became erroneously known as the Jerusalem artichoke.

Jerusalem artichokes were popular during the seventeenth century and no explanations about them were required. Then over a century ago, the affection for these gnarled tubers waned.

Like some other unfamiliar items, the Jerusalem artichoke needed a name change to enhance its consumer appeal. They are now frequently marketed as sunchokes or as sunroots. These names more aptly describe their heritage as members of the sunflower family.

Raw sunchokes are crisp and crunchy like water chestnuts, with a sweet, delicate flavor. When cooked, the flesh becomes tender and moist.

AVAILABILITY: Year round, but supplies are at their sweetest during the fall and winter months.

SELECTION AND STORAGE: Chokes vary in size and color. They are predominantly tan or golden-brown, but they can also be tinged with red or purple. Look for firm, clean tubers of equal size so they will cook evenly. Select those as smooth as possible for easier cleaning. Avoid any sprouting tubers or those tinged with green.

At home, chokes can be stored in a cool, dry, well-ventilated area or refrigerated in plastic for maximum shelf life. They will keep for a week or more if refrigerated.

PREPARATION: Jerusalem artichokes do not require peeling, although you may choose to do so depending on the recipe. The gnarled knobs make peeling between the crevices difficult. You can scrub them with a vegetable brush. If you peel or cut the chokes, be sure to plunge them immediately into cold water and add a little lemon juice or vinegar to prevent darkening.

Allow 1–1½ pounds of sunchokes for 4 servings. One pound raw sunchokes equals 3 cups sliced and 2½ cups when cooked and peeled.

To boil: Cook whole sunchokes in boiling water for 12–25 minutes, depending on size. Avoid overcooking which makes them mushy.

To steam: Small sunchokes will become tender steamed over a small amount of boiling water in 8–15 minutes. Larger tubers require longer cooking. Avoid overcooking which makes them mushy.

To microwave: Prick chokes and cook on high power. One pound chokes should cook in 5–6 minutes.

To bake: Lightly baste whole unpeeled chokes with oil. Bake chokes at 400° F. Medium-size chokes should cook in about 20 minutes.

SERVING SUGGESTIONS: The sunchoke's crisp, white flesh is excellent raw, sliced into salads, marinated, or served as a dip accompaniment.

- Serve puréed in soups.
- Roast along with meat, adding them to the roasting pan the last 30 minutes of cooking. Baste with the pan drippings.
- Marinate raw chokes in a vinaigrette and serve as a crisp salad.
- Serve cooked chokes with lemon butter or margarine and a sprinkling of minced fresh herbs.

NUTRITION INFORMATION: Sunchokes provide iron and vitamin C as well as other nutrients. The calorie content varies according to the length of storage. A ½-cup serving has about 57 calories. As storage time increases, so does the calorie count.

HEARTY CHICKEN VEGETABLE SOUP

2 quarts water	½ teaspoon pepper
1 whole chicken, 3 to 4 pounds	1 tablespoon chopped fresh parsley
2 medium onions	1 teaspoon dried basil
2 cups sliced celery	1 pound sunchokes
2 teaspoons salt	3 large carrots

Place the water and chicken in a large kettle. Peel and slice the onions. Add the onion, celery, seasonings, and herbs to the kettle.

Simmer covered for 30 minutes. Scrub the sunchokes and dice. Scrape carrots and cut into thin slices. Add the sunchokes and carrots to the soup. Simmer for an additional 30–40 minutes, or until the chicken is tender.

Remove the chicken from the soup and place on a cutting board to cool slightly. Remove the meat from the bones, discarding skin and bones. Dice chicken and return to soup. Taste, adjusting seasoning if necessary. Serve hot.

MAKES 8 SERVINGS

SUNCHOKE PATTIES

1 pound sunchokes
1/2 cup chopped onion
1 egg
3 tablespoons flour

1/2 teaspoon salt
1/4 teaspoon pepper
2 tablespoons margarine or butter

Cook whole sunchokes in boiling water for 10–20 minutes, or until tender. Shred cooked sunchokes and place in a medium mixing bowl. Combine onion, egg, flour, and seasonings, mixing well. In a medium skillet, melt the margarine or butter. Divide sunchoke mixture into 4 portions. Place in the skillet and flatten into pancakes. Cook until browned on one side; turn and brown on the other side, adding more margarine or butter if needed. Serve hot.

MAKES 4 SERVINGS

SHREDDED SUNCHOKE SALAD

2¹/₂ tablespoons Dijon
    mustard
2 tablespoons vegetable
    oil

¹/₂ cup dairy sour cream or
    plain yogurt
Salt and pepper
1 pound sunchokes

In a medium bowl, combine the mustard, oil, and sour cream or yogurt. Whip the mixture with a wire whisk. Season with salt and pepper to taste. Peel the sunchokes, if desired, and shred them. Immediately add shredded sunchokes to the mustard and sour-cream or yogurt sauce. Toss to coat.

MAKES 4 SERVINGS

CREAMY MUSHROOM AND
SUNCHOKE SOUP

1 tablespoon fresh lemon or
    lime juice
1 pound sunchokes
2 garlic cloves
1 large onion
5 tablespoons margarine or
    butter, divided

3 cups chicken stock or broth
1 pound fresh mushrooms
1 cup light cream
Salt and pepper
2 scallions

Fill a bowl with 2 cups water; add lemon or lime juice. Peel the sunchokes, cut into thin slices, and plunge into the bowl.

Peel and mince garlic. Peel and chop the onion. Melt 2 tablespoons margarine or butter in a large saucepan. Add garlic and onion; sauté over medium heat about 5 minutes or until tender.

Drain the sunchokes. Add the sunchokes and the chicken stock to the saucepan; cover and simmer 15–20 minutes or until the sunchokes are tender. Remove sunchokes from heat. Purée mixture in a food processor and return to saucepan.

Meanwhile, wipe mushrooms with a damp cloth, trim stems, and slice mushrooms. In a skillet, melt remaining 3 tablespoons margarine or butter; add the mushrooms and sauté about 3 minutes or until tender. Add mushrooms and cream to the soup and heat through. Season with salt and pepper to taste. Transfer soup to a soup tureen or individual bowls. Thinly slice scallions and use to garnish soup.

MAKES 4 TO 6 SERVINGS

JÍCAMA

Jícama (pronounced heé-ka-mah), a member of the morning glory family, is the underground tuber of a leguminous vine. It is as familiar to Mexican tables as the potato is to American tables.

One of the species, Pachyrhizus erosus, *jícama originated in Mexico. The Spanish introduced jícama to the Philippines during the seventeenth century, where it became popular with the Chinese and then continued to attract fanciers throughout Asia and the Pacific.*

Jícama resembles a flattened turnip in shape, although

some have furrows on all four sides and look like four-leaf clovers. Jícamas range in size from as small as a ¹/2 pound to as large as 6 pounds!

Jícama's crunchy-crisp flesh has a mild taste with a touch of sweetness. Its refreshing, juicy flesh is excellent raw, splashed with a little fresh lime juice for extra zest. The firm, crisp texture of jícama is retained throughout cooking.

AVAILABILITY: Year round.

SELECTION AND STORAGE: Choose firm tubers, free of blemishes. Those that are heavy-skinned may tend to be fibrous and starchy. Whole jícama can be stored unwrapped in a cool, dark, dry place or in the refrigerator for several weeks. Cut jícama should be wrapped in plastic, stored in the refrigerator, and used within a week.

PREPARATION: Jícama requires peeling for any purpose. Cut into chunks as needed, then using a paring knife, remove the skin and fibrous underlayer. Cut, slice, dice, shred, or cut into julienne strips, as desired. A one pound jícama yields about 3 cups chopped or shredded flesh.

SERVING SUGGESTIONS:
- A traditional Mexican use of jícama is to sprinkle slices or sticks with chili powder, lime juice, and salt.
- Use as a water chestnut substitute if fresh ones aren't available.
- Toss into fruit, vegetable, poultry, or seafood salads.
- Serve as an accompaniment with dips.
- Add to stir-frys.
- Marinate jícama for extra flavor.

NUTRITION INFORMATION: A 3¹/2-ounce serving is low in sodium and a good source of vitamin C, supplies potassium, and contains about 45 calories.

SWEET-AND-SOUR PORK

1 pound boneless pork
2 tablespoons dry white wine
2 tablespoons reduced-
   sodium soy sauce
2 medium carrots
2 medium green peppers
1 garlic clove
1 medium onion

1/4 pound jícama
1 cup diced fresh pineapple
1 egg
3 tablespoons flour
1 tablespoon cornstarch
1/4 cup plus 2 tablespoons
   peanut oil
   Hot cooked rice

SWEET-AND-SOUR SAUCE II

1/2 cup brown sugar
1/2 cup white vinegar
1/4 cup water
2 tablespoons cornstarch

2 tablespoons reduced-
   sodium soy sauce
1 tablespoon dry white wine

Trim fat from pork and cut meat into 1-inch cubes. Place pork, wine, and soy sauce in a bowl. Cover and marinate for at least 1 hour.

While pork is marinating, prepare the vegetables. Scrape carrots and cut into thin diagonal slices. Remove seeds and membrane from peppers; cut peppers into 1-inch pieces. Peel and mince the garlic. Peel onion and cut into thin slices. Peel and dice the jícama. Set the vegetables and pineapple aside.

After pork has marinated, pour off the marinade. In a medium bowl, beat the egg. Stir in the flour and cornstarch and mix until smooth. Dip pork into batter and thoroughly coat. Heat 1/4 cup oil in a large skillet or wok. Add pork and cook over medium-high heat for about 8 minutes, or until done. Remove pork from skillet and keep warm. In a small bowl, combine the sauce ingredients and set aside.

Pour off drippings from skillet and replace with remaining 2 tablespoons oil. Heat oil; add carrots, peppers, and garlic; sauté for 4 minutes. Add onion and jícama; sauté for an additional 2 minutes. Add the pineapple, cooked pork, and reserved sauce. Cook the mixture until the sauce is thickened. Serve over hot cooked rice.

MAKES 4 TO 5 SERVINGS

POLYNESIAN MEATBALLS WITH SOY WALNUTS

Meatballs are coated with a light batter, simmered with pineapple and crunchy jícama, then garnished with walnuts.

1 pound ground beef
1/2 cup minced onion
1/2 cup chopped walnuts
1/2 cup fine dry bread crumbs
1/4 cup milk
1/4 teaspoon salt
   Pinch of black pepper
3 eggs
3/4 cup flour
1/4 cup vegetable oil
3/4 cup white wine

3/4 cup beef stock
1 cup diced fresh pineapple
1/2 cup peeled and diced jícama
2 tablespoons cornstarch
1/4 cup sugar
1/4 cup white vinegar
1 tablespoon reduced-sodium soy sauce
Soy Walnuts (recipe follows)
Hot cooked rice

SOY WALNUTS

1 tablespoon margarine or butter

1 tablespoon reduced-sodium soy sauce
1/2 cup chopped walnuts

In a mixing bowl, combine ground beef, onion, chopped walnuts, bread crumbs, milk, salt, and pepper. Mix well and form into 12 meatballs. In a small bowl, beat the eggs. Add flour and stir until smooth. Dip meatballs into batter and coat well.

Heat oil in a large skillet. Add meatballs and cook over medium heat until meatballs are done and batter is golden brown. Pour off drippings. Add wine, stock, pineapple, and jícama to skillet and simmer uncovered for about 5 minutes.

Meanwhile, prepare Soy Walnuts. In a small skillet, melt the margarine or butter. Add soy sauce and walnuts. Sauté for about 3 minutes.

In a cup, mix together cornstarch, sugar, vinegar, and soy sauce and blend until smooth. Stir into meatball mixture and cook until thickened. Garnish with Soy Walnuts. Serve over rice.

MAKES 4 SERVINGS

CELERY AND JÍCAMA CRUNCH

1 bunch of celery, about 1 pound

1 1/4 cups chicken stock or broth

1/2 teaspoon dried basil

2 tablespoons cornstarch

1 1/2 cups peeled and diced jícama

3 tablespoons margarine or butter

2/3 cup fine dry bread crumbs

1/2 cup sliced almonds

Trim leaves and cut off base of celery. Cut ribs diagonally into slices about 1/2-inch thick and measure about 2 1/2 cups. Set aside. In a large saucepan combine the celery, broth, and basil. Bring the mixture to a boil, cover, and cook over medium heat for about 10 minutes. Remove from heat.

In a cup combine cornstarch with about ¹/₄ cup broth; blend until smooth. Gradually stir the cornstarch mixture into the hot broth. Add jícama. Cook mixture for 1–2 minutes, until thickened. Pour mixture into a lightly oiled 1-quart casserole. Set aside.

In a small skillet, melt the margarine or butter. Add the bread crumbs and almonds. Toss to coat. Sprinkle crumb mixture over vegetables. Bake uncovered in preheated 350° F oven for 25–30 minutes, until topping is golden brown and sauce is bubbly.

MAKES 6 SERVINGS

MEXICALI SALAD

¹/₂ pound jícama
1 medium green pepper
³/₄ cup chopped red onion
1 medium cucumber
¹/₄ cup white wine vinegar
3 tablespoons olive oil

1 tablespoon chopped fresh
    oregano or ³/₄ teaspoon
    dried oregano
¹/₂ teaspoon salt
¹/₄ teaspoon black pepper

Peel and dice the jícama. Measure enough diced jícama to equal about 2 cups. Remove seeds and membrane from pepper; chop the pepper. Peel and slice the cucumber. Combine vegetables in a mixing bowl. Mix vinegar, oil, oregano, salt, and pepper together. Pour the mixture over the vegetables. Toss to coat. Cover and chill for at least 1 hour.

MAKES 4 TO 6 SERVINGS

HEAVENLY JÍCAMA

Jícama's slightly sweet flavor combines deliciously with fruit.

1 pound jícama
1 cup shredded coconut
3/4 cup raisins
1/2 cup mayonnaise
2 tablespoons sugar

1 tablespoon fresh lemon or
  lime juice
2 teaspoons grated lemon or
  lime peel

Peel and shred jícama and measure 3 cups. In a mixing bowl, combine jícama, coconut, and raisins. In a small bowl, combine mayonnaise, sugar, lemon or lime juice, and peel; blend well. Pour mixture over jícama and toss to coat.

MAKES 4 TO 6 SERVINGS

VARIATIONS:: Add halved grapes or chunks of fresh pineapple, apples, or pears.

JÍCAMA, STRAWBERRY, AND TOASTED PECAN SALAD

1/4 cup chopped pecans
3/4 pound jícama
2 bunches watercress
1 cup sliced fresh
  strawberries

*Strawberry-Poppy Seed
Vinaigrette (recipe follows)*

Preheat oven to 400° F. Place pecans in a pie plate and toast in the oven about 3–4 minutes or until toasted. Set pecans aside to cool.

Peel and cut jícama into julienne sticks, about ⅛-inch thick and 2–3 inches long (there should be about 3 cups). Wash watercress, discard thick stems; pat dry. Divide watercress among 4 salad plates. Pile about ¾ cup julienned jícama over the watercress on each plate; arrange strawberries over salad. Sprinkle 1 tablespoon toasted pecans over each salad. Serve with Strawberry-Poppy Seed Vinaigrette.

MAKES 4 SERVINGS

STRAWBERRY-POPPY SEED VINAIGRETTE

3 tablespoons strawberry
　vinegar
2 tablespoons sugar
1 tablespoon chopped onion

¼ teaspoon salt
⅓ cup vegetable oil
1 teaspoon poppy seeds

Combine vinegar, sugar, onion, and salt in a blender. Whirl until smooth. Add oil and whirl until thickened. Stir in poppy seeds. Refrigerate any remaining dressing.

MAKES ABOUT ⅔ CUP

$\mathcal{K}$IWIFRUIT

The brown, suedelike-skinned kiwifruit has become a produce basic, captivating consumers with its dazzling emerald green color and exquisite flavor. The taste of kiwifruit is as unique as its natural packaging. It has a tangy, tart-sweet combination of other fruit flavors, such as strawberry and melon, yet its taste is truly one of a kind.

Grown since ancient times in China, it was introduced into New Zealand in 1906 by a missionary, where it soon began commercial cultivation. For years this fruit was marketed as the Chinese gooseberry. Then, in the early 1970s, it was renamed the kiwifruit after the native New Zealand bird, the kiwi. The new name seemed to suit this fuzzy little fruit perfectly, and good promotion and marketing helped kiwi sales take off.

Kiwifruit was actually grown in California as early as the 1930s, long before it became one of the darlings of the produce industry. During the 1960s, commercial vineyard cultivation was established in the state.

Availability: Year round, with supplies from California from October through May and from New Zealand from June through October.

Selection and Storage: Kiwifruit is often displayed rather firm, so it should be given additional ripening time at home. Keep fruit at room temperature until it yields to palm pressure when gently squeezed. To hasten ripening, place fruit in a basket or in a paper bag with an apple or banana and store until ripe. Once ripe, kiwifruit can be refrigerated for many weeks.

Preparation: Kiwifruit can be enjoyed simply halved and scooped with a spoon. Its bright green flesh, studded with tiny black edible seeds, is stunning peeled and sliced, used in salads, desserts, with entrées, and as a glittering garnish.

Kiwifruit contains an enzyme that serves as a perfect meat tenderizer and flavor enhancer. To use as a tenderizer, purée the fruit and spread it over meat that has been pricked with a knife or fork. Allow it to stand about 30 minutes before cooking.

This enzyme also prevents gelatin from setting, as do enzymes from pineapple and papaya. Therefore, if you plan to use fresh kiwis in gelatin recipes, be sure to cook them briefly to inactivate the enzyme. Cooking, however, will affect the intensity of the kiwis bright green color.

Because of the enzyme is able to break down protein, be careful when combining fresh kiwifruit with milk or milk products. Be sure to cook the fruit before mixing with milk products, unless you plan to use the prepared food or drink right away.

Serving Suggestions:

- Add slices to fresh fruit or poultry salads.
- Top cereals with kiwi.

- Arrange glistening, lightly glazed slices over cheesecake or tarts.
- Blend kiwi into frothy fresh fruit blender drinks.
- Garnish poultry and meat dishes.
- Purée kiwi for refreshing ices or sorbets.
- Fill meringue shells with sweetened whipped cream and top with kiwi for a dazzling dessert.

NUTRITION INFORMATION: An average kiwifruit is an excellent source of vitamin C; provides potassium, important minerals, and fiber; is low in sodium; and contains about 55 calories.

KIWI VEAL AMANDINE

Toasted almonds and kiwifruits add the crowning touch to this quick, yet elegant dish.

5 tablespoons margarine or butter, divided	Salt and pepper
1/2 cup sliced almonds	2 garlic cloves
1 pound thin-sliced veal	2 kiwifruits
1/2 cup flour	1/3 cup brandy

In a large skillet, melt 1 tablespoon margarine or butter. Add the almonds and sauté until lightly toasted. Remove almonds from the skillet and set aside.

Pound the veal with a meat mallet. Dredge with flour seasoned with salt and pepper. Peel and mince the garlic cloves. Peel and slice the kiwifruits. Melt remaining 4 tablespoons margarine or butter in the skillet. Add the garlic and veal and sauté over medium-high heat for about 5 minutes, browning on both sides. If the skillet is not large enough to hold all the slices at one time, sauté as many slices as will fit in the skillet in one layer, with half of the garlic; then remove them from the skillet and keep warm. Melt more margarine or butter; add the rest of the garlic, and sauté remaining veal in the same fashion.

When the veal is browned, add the kiwi slices and pour brandy over veal and kiwis. Cook for 1–2 minutes, or just until the kiwis are heated through. Remove from heat and garnish with the toasted almonds.

MAKES 4 SERVINGS

KIWI CREAM MERINGUE

An almond-studded meringue cake is layered with whipped cream and sliced kiwis.

4 tablespoons margarine or
  butter, softened
1/2 cup plus 2 tablespoons
  sugar
4 eggs, separated
1 teaspoon vanilla extract
1 cup sifted all-purpose
  flour
1 teaspoon baking powder

1/4 teaspoon salt
1/3 cup light cream or
  evaporated milk
  Meringue Topping
  (recipe follows)
1/3 cup sliced almonds
1 1/2 cups heavy cream
1/2 teaspoon almond extract
6 kiwifruits

In a medium mixing bowl, cream together margarine or butter and 1/2 cup sugar. Separate eggs. Add egg yolks, one at a time, beating well after each addition; add vanilla. Reserve whites for Meringue Topping.

Sift together flour, baking powder, and salt. Alternate adding the dry ingredients and evaporated milk to the creamed mixture. Spread mixture in 2 buttered 8-inch cake pans. Top with Meringue Topping. On one layer only, sprinkle almonds over meringue. Bake both layers at 325° F for 35–40 minutes. Remove from oven and cool.

At serving time, whip cream until stiff. Add remaining 2 tablespoons sugar and almond extract; beat to blend. Peel and slice kiwifruits.

Place the layer without almonds meringue side down. Spread whipped cream on top. Arrange 3 sliced kiwifruits over cream. Place almond layer on top, meringue side up. Spread remaining cream on meringue. Garnish with remaining kiwi slices.

MAKES 8 SERVINGS

MERINGUE TOPPING

4 egg whites   *1 teaspoon vanilla extract*
1 cup sugar

In a medium bowl, beat egg whites until stiff. Gradually add sugar, beating well after each addition. Add vanilla and beat to blend.

JEWEL PIE

This pie glistens like jewels. A gem of a dessert!

Cookie Crust (*recipe
follows*)
1 quart strawberries (about
2 pounds)
5 medium kiwifruits

$^3/_4$ cup sugar
$^1/_4$ cup cornstarch
1 cup water
1 tablespoon orange liqueur
Whipped cream

Prepare and bake the cookie crust. Rinse and hull strawberries, keeping them whole. Peel and slice kiwifruits. Place berries and kiwifruits in a large mixing bowl, reserving 5 medium berries. Set aside.

In a small saucepan, combine sugar and cornstarch. Gradually add water and stir to blend. Cook over medium heat, stirring constantly, until mixture is thickened and clear. Remove from heat. Purée reserved berries and stir into glaze. Add liqueur and stir to blend. Pour mixture over fruit and gently toss to coat. Turn into prepared cookie crust. Chill for at least 4 hours. Serve with a dollop of whipped cream.

MAKES 6 SERVINGS

COOKIE CRUST

4 tablespoons margarine or
butter, softened
$^1/_4$ cup sugar

1 egg yolk
1 cup all-purpose flour

In a mixing bowl, cream the margarine or butter and sugar together. Beat the egg yolk and add to the creamed mixture. Add the flour and mix until crumbly, using a pastry blender or 2 knives scissor-fashion. Press mixture into a 9-inch pie plate. Bake at 400° F for 8–10 minutes, until the edges are lightly browned. Cool before filling.

KIWI SABAYON

A fluffy dessert sauce laced with wine or sherry blankets these fruit jewels.

4 egg yolks
3/4 cup sugar
3/4 cup dry white wine or
   sherry
Cracked ice

1/3 cup heavy cream
6 kiwifruits
2 fresh peaches or
   nectarines*

In the top part of a double boiler, combine egg yolks, sugar, and white wine or sherry. Using a wire whisk, beat vigorously over boiling water until thickened, about 5 minutes. Remove from heat and set top part of double boiler in a large bowl of cracked ice. Beat mixture until it cools, 4–5 minutes. Whip cream until stiff and fold into sauce. Pour into a covered container and chill.

To serve, slice fruits and place in individual sherbet glasses. Pour sauce over fruit and serve. Any remaining sauce can be refrigerated. Sauce will keep for several days or more.

MAKES 8 SERVINGS

* Additional kiwis may be substituted for the peaches or nectarines.

KIWI SMOOTHIE

2 kiwifruits
2 large bananas
1 cup fresh orange juice

8–10 ice cubes
2 tablespoons honey

Peel the kiwis and bananas and coarsely chop them. In a blender or food processor, combine all the ingredients and mix until well-blended.

MAKES 4 CUPS

KIWI DAIQUIRI

2 kiwifruits
1/3 cup fresh lime juice
2 1/2 tablespoons sugar

1/4 cup light rum
6 ice cubes

Peel the kiwis and coarsely chop them. In a blender or food processor, combine all the ingredients and mix until well-blended.

MAKES 2 SERVINGS

$\mathcal{K}$OHLRABI

Somewhat like a turnip in size and shape, kohlrabi is actually a thickened stem that grows above ground. Its name is adopted from the German kohl, *meaning 'cabbage,' and* rabi, *meaning 'turnip.' The cabbage turnip is a member of the* Brassica *species, and its relatives include rutabaga, broccoli, and cauliflower among others.*

Its flavor is mild, with hints of broccoli and radish. Kohlrabi's globe-shaped bulb is sweet, crisp, and juicy, and can be either light green or magenta. Kohlrabi leaves appear turniplike and taste similar to kale or spinach with a sharper bite.

Kohlrabi originated in northern Europe in the sixteenth century. Today it is familiar to cooks in many European countries, Israel, Russia, China, and in American communities with a heritage from these areas.

AVAILABILITY: Kohlrabi is chiefly available from spring through early fall, in peak supply during early summer, but appears in produce departments throughout the year.

SELECTION AND STORAGE: Choose small to medium bulbs, no larger than $2^{1}/_{2}$ inches in diameter, for the sweetest, most tender eating. Larger bulbs tend to be fibrous, tough, and bitter. If the tops are attached, they should be green and fresh-looking. A pound of trimmed kohlrabi should serve 3 or 4 people. At home, separate the leaves from the bulbs. Wrap in plastic and refrigerate. The leaves should be used within a few days; the bulbs within a week.

PREPARATION: Cut the stems from the bulb. Tiny kohlrabies do not need peeling, but all other sizes require peeling to remove the thicker skin and fibrous underlayer beneath the skin. If desired, the peel can be kept on for cooking and removed after cooking.

The crisp flesh can be served raw in salads, as a relish, or as a crunchy accompaniment to dips. The bulbs can be sliced, cut into quarters, cubes, or julienne strips and cooked until crisp-tender.

To boil: Place trimmed bulbs in a saucepan, cover with boiling water, and boil gently until tender, about 25–30 minutes.

Kohlrabi leaves can be cooked in a large, covered pot of boiling water for just 2–3 minutes or until tender. They can also be prepared by sautéing in oil until tender.

To microwave: Place in a microwaveable dish with a few tablespoons water. Four whole bulbs, about 2½ inches in diameter, will microcook in 7–9 minutes on high power.

SERVING SUGGESTIONS:

- Serve raw or blanched and chilled kohlrabi in a vinaigrette or creamy dressing.
- Combine with carrots or winter squash.
- Grate or shred into coleslaws.
- Sauté and season with curry or dill.
- Toss cooked slices with lemon butter or margarine.
- Serve cooked kohlrabi in a hollandaise, cheese, or cream sauce.

Nutrition Information: One cup is an excellent source of vitamin C, provides potassium and fiber, is low in sodium, and has about 40 calories.

KOHLRABI AND CARROT CASSEROLE

4 medium kohlrabi bulbs
5 medium carrots
4 tablespoons margarine or
    butter, divided
1/2 cup chopped onion

2 tablespoons flour
1 1/3 cups milk
1/2 teaspoon salt
    Pinch of black pepper
3/4 cup soft bread crumbs

Peel and slice the kohlrabies. In a large saucepan, cook kohlrabies in boiling salted water for 5–8 minutes. Scrape carrots and cut into thin bias-cut slices. Add carrots to kohlrabies and cook for another 10 minutes, or until vegetables are tender.

While vegetables are cooking, melt 2 tablespoons margarine or butter in a medium saucepan. Add onion and sauté until tender. Add flour and stir until well-blended. Gradually stir in milk and seasonings and cook until thickened. Drain vegetables. Pour white sauce over vegetables. Turn into a buttered 1-quart casserole.

Melt remaining margarine or butter; add bread crumbs, and toss to coat. Sprinkle bread crumbs on top of vegetables. Bake uncovered at 350° F for 20–25 minutes, or until lightly browned.

MAKES 6 SERVINGS

KOHLRABI COLESLAW

4 medium kohlrabi bulbs
2 medium carrots
1 medium green or red
    pepper
1/2 cup minced celery
1/3 cup minced onion

2/3 cup mayonnaise
1 tablespoon fresh lemon
    juice
1 teaspoon sugar
1/4 teaspoon salt
1/4 teaspoon pepper

Peel and shred the kohlrabi bulbs; measure enough for about 3 cups. Scrape and grate the carrots. Remove seeds and membrane from pepper; mince the pepper. In a large bowl, combine all the vegetables. In a small bowl, combine mayonnaise, lemon juice, sugar, and seasonings, blending well. Pour over vegetable mixture and toss to coat. Cover and chill.

MAKES 6 SERVINGS

KUMQUAT

The Chinese phrase Chin kan, meaning "gold orange," aptly describes this tiny fruit that resembles a miniature orange. Although closely related to citrus, the kumquat has its own genus, Fortunella. It was named after Robert Fortune, a plant explorer for the London Horticultural Society who introduced it into Europe in the mid-nineteenth century. Around 1885, the kumquat plant was brought from Japan to the United States and today is cultivated in Florida as well as China, Japan, and Taiwan.

Kumquats are golden yellow to reddish-orange, oblong or round. They are unique in that the peel is sweet and the pulp is tart.

Sometimes kumquats are marketed still attached to sprigs of dark green, mandarinlike leaves. The contrast of the petite orange fruits with the deep green leaves makes them an attractive fruit bowl decoration. This eleventh-century Chinese description glorified the kumquat's decorative value: "When served on the table they glisten like golden bullets." In fact, it was a Chinese custom to set a small kumquat plant on the dining table, not only for decoration, but also to be eaten.

AVAILABILITY: December to May, with peak supplies in early winter.

SELECTION AND STORAGE: Select firm, bright, and glossy fruit. Kumquats can be kept at room temperature, but refrigeration prolongs their shelf life. When refrigerated, kumquats will last several weeks.

PREPARATION: If serving raw, blanching kumquats helps to soften the skin and bring them to their juiciness. Plunge kumquats into boiling water for about 20 seconds. Kumquats contain seeds, so unless they're kept whole, the seeds should to be removed. Slice, halve, or quarter the kumquats, depending on the particular recipe, and use a knife tip to remove the seeds.

SERVING SUGGESTIONS:

- Thinly slice and use in fresh fruit, vegetable, meat, or poultry salads.
- Use as a tangy addition to meat and vegetable recipes.
- Poach in a sugar syrup and serve as a meat accompaniment.
- Make marmalade, preserves, or jam.
- Garnish cocktails with kumquats.

NUTRITION INFORMATION: One kumquat provides vitamin C and potassium, is low in sodium, and contains 12 calories.

STUFFED PORK CHOPS WITH KUMQUAT-RAISIN SAUCE

Browned and simmered in fresh orange juice with raisins and kumquats, these tender stuffed chops make a hearty winter treat.

1 tablespoon margarine or butter	Salt and pepper
1/2 cup raisins, divided	1 tablespoon vegetable oil
1/2 cup chopped celery	1 1/2 cups fresh orange juice, divided
1/4 cup chopped onion	1 1/4 cups water, divided
1 cup seasoned stuffing mix	3 tablespoons honey
1/4 cup hot water	1/2 cup halved and seeded kumquats
4 double pork chops with pockets for stuffing	1 tablespoon cornstarch

In a small skillet, melt the margarine or butter. Combine 1/4 cup raisins, the celery, and onion; sauté until tender. Add the stuffing mix and water; mix well. Set aside.

Season chops with salt and pepper. In a large skillet, brown chops in the oil over medium heat. Pour off pork drippings. Fill chops with stuffing mixture and secure with wooden picks. Combine 3/4 cup orange juice, 3/4 cup water, honey, and kumquats. Add to chops. Simmer, covered, for about 1 hour, adding remaining liquid as needed. Spoon mixture over chops occasionally.

About 5 minutes before serving, add remaining raisins to gravy. Place cornstarch in a small bowl, and slowly stir in 1/4 cup gravy, blending until smooth. Add to chops and stir until thickened. To serve, spoon gravy over chops.

MAKES 4 SERVINGS

KUMQUAT CHICKEN ORIENTAL

6 ounces fresh kumquats	3 tablespoons margarine
3/4 cup water	1/4 cup fresh orange juice
1/3 cup sugar	2 tablespoons honey
1 1/2 pounds boneless,	3 tablespoons reduced-
skinless chicken breasts	sodium soy sauce
1/4 cup flour	2 teaspoons cornstarch
1 1/2 teaspoons paprika	

Trim ends from kumquats and cut crosswise into 1/4-inch slices; remove seeds. In a small saucepan, combine kumquats, water, and sugar. Bring to a boil and simmer uncovered for about 15 minutes, or until syrup is slightly thickened.

While kumquat mixture is simmering, pound chicken with a meat mallet. In a small bowl, combine flour and paprika. Dredge chicken with flour mixture. In a medium skillet, melt the margarine and add chicken. Cook over medium heat for about 6–8 minutes, turning chicken on both sides to brown lightly. Place chicken in a shallow, lightly oiled baking dish. Set aside.

Combine orange juice, honey, and soy sauce; stir into the kumquat mixture. Pour kumquat sauce over chicken. Bake uncovered in preheated 375° F oven for 25–30 minutes, or until chicken is done. Remove from oven. Drain sauce from pan and place in a small saucepan. Keep chicken warm.

In a small cup, dissolve cornstarch in about 2 tablespoons of the kumquat sauce. Pour into the saucepan and cook over medium heat until sauce is thickened. Spoon kumquat sauce over chicken and serve hot.

MAKES 4 SERVINGS

RUGULA

ATEMOYA

SIAN PEARS

BOK CHOY

PRICKLY PEAR

CARAMBOLA

CHAYOTE

HILI PEPPERS

CHINESE CABBAGE
CELERY CABBAGE

EIJOA

FENNEL

GINGERROOT

JERUSALEM ARTICHOKES

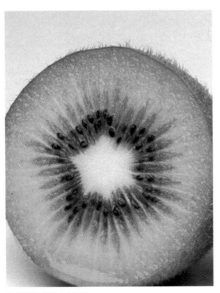

KIWIFRUIT

KOHLRABI

LYCHEES

KUMQUAT

MAMEY SAPOTE

MANGO

PAPAYA

PASSION FRUIT

PERSIMMON

PLANTAIN

POMEGRANATE

QUINCE

RHUBARB

SUGAR SNAP PEAS

SPAGHETTI SQUASH

ALFALFA SPROUTS
BEAN SPROUTS

CILANTRO / JICAMA / CHAYOTE / TOMATILLO

KUMQUAT GLAZE

1/2 cup coarsely chopped
   kumquats
1/2 cup light corn syrup
1/2 cup light brown sugar

1/2 cup water
1 tablespoon prepared
   mustard

In a small saucepan, combine all ingredients. Boil for about 10 minutes, stirring frequently. Use as a glaze for ham, pork, or poultry.

MAKES 1 CUP

HARVEST SQUASH

3 medium acorn squash
6 tablespoons brown sugar
3 tablespoons margarine or
   butter

10 kumquats

Cut the squash lengthwise into halves and scoop out the seeds and stringy pulp. Fill each center with 1 tablespoon brown sugar and 1/2 tablespoon margarine or butter. Cut the kumquats into 1/8-inch slices and remove the seeds. Divide kumquat slices among the squash halves. Place squash halves in a shallow baking pan containing 1/4 inch of water. Bake uncovered at 400° F for about 50 minutes, or until squashes are tender.

MAKES 6 SERVINGS

KUMQUAT DESSERT SAUCE

1 pound fresh kumquats
1/2 cup water
1 cup sugar

3 tablespoons light corn syrup
2 tablespoons orange liqueur

Wash kumquats, cut into thin slices, and remove the seeds. Pour water into a medium saucepan and cook over medium heat for 10–12 minutes, or until tender. Add the sugar and corn syrup and cook for 5–8 minutes, until the mixture thickens. Add the liqueur and mix well. Serve warm, spooned over pound or sponge cake; or chilled over ice cream.

MAKES 2 CUPS

*L*EEKS

The leek is an exceptionally sweet and mild member of the onion family, particularly valued as a subtle, yet irresistible flavoring ingredient.

The exact origin of the leek is unknown, but ancient varieties are believed to have been more bulbous than today's varieties. The Egyptians introduced the leek to the ancient Romans, who in turn introduced it to the English. Later the leek became the national emblem of the Welsh to commemorate their important victory over the Saxons in 640 A.D. At the advice of St. David, Welsh soldiers wore a leek in their caps during battle so they could identify their comrades. The tradition has been carried on since then, for every March 1st on St. David's Day, the Welsh proudly wear leeks to celebrate the victory.

Looking like an enlarged version of the green onion or scallion, leeks have a thickened white base about 1–2 inches in diameter which extends into broad, flattened green leaves. The bulb and tender portion of the light green leaves are the parts that are prepared.

AVAILABILITY: Year round.

SELECTION AND STORAGE: Choose leeks that are well-blanched 2–3 inches from the base and have fresh-looking leaves. Small- to medium-size leeks, less than 1 1/2 inches in diameter, are the most tender; larger ones tend to be tough. Keep refrigerated in a plastic bag and use within a week.

PREPARATION: Trim off the root ends and discard. Leeks should be thoroughly washed to remove grit and sand which accumulates under the outer layers. Discard coarse outer leaves. Trim tops keeping about 2–3 inches of the pale green leaves. For easier cleaning, split the leek in half lengthwise, cutting to within 1/2 inch of the root end, if leeks are to be kept whole. Otherwise, the leek can be fully split. Rinse thoroughly under cold running water.

Leeks can be eaten raw or cooked. Keep cooking time to a minimum since overcooking makes them mushy.

To boil: Place leeks in a skillet, with $1/2$ inch boiling water. Cover and cook about 4–7 minutes or just until tender.

To microwave: For $1^1/2$ pounds of trimmed and halved leeks, arrange leeks in a single layer in a microwaveable baking dish with only the water that clings to them after rinsing. Cover and microwave on high power 4–5 minutes, rotating the dish halfway through cooking. Allow to stand 5 minutes.

To stir-fry: Cut white portions into thin slices. Heat a little vegetable oil in a skillet and sauté about 1 minute. Add a few tablespoons water or chicken stock, cover, and cook 2–3 minutes or until crisp-tender.

SERVING SUGGESTIONS:

- Serve au gratin or creamed.
- Use in classic soup recipes featuring leeks, such as Vichyssoise or Cock-a-Leekie.
- Season hot cooked leeks with fresh herbs and a splash of lemon butter or margarine.
- Sprinkle cooked leeks with grated lemon peel.
- Use raw in salads or serve alone with a vinaigrette.

NUTRITION INFORMATION: One leek provides potassium, iron, and some vitamin C; is low in sodium; and has less than 40 calories.

POACHED RED SNAPPER WITH LEEKS

6 shallots

3 medium tomatoes

5 leeks, bulbs only

2 tablespoons margarine or
  butter

Juice of 1 lemon

2 red snapper fillets, skin on,
  about 2 pounds

$^1/_4$ teaspoon salt

$^1/_4$ teaspoon pepper

2 cups chablis or other dry
  white wine

$^1/_4$ cup chopped fresh parsley
  Paprika

Peel and mince shallots. Peel, seed, and chop tomatoes. Cut leeks (bulbs only) into 2-inch pieces; slice lengthwise into julienne strips.

Melt margarine or butter in skillet large enough to hold fillets without overlapping. Add lemon juice, shallots, and fillets, skin side down. Season with salt and pepper. Add leeks and wine. Bring to a boil, reduce heat, cover, and simmer for 10–12 minutes or until fish flakes when tested with a fork. With slotted spatula, carefully lift fillets to heated serving platter or warm plates and keep warm.

Cook liquid uncovered, over high heat until sauce is reduced by half. Add tomatoes and cook 3 minutes. Pour over fillets. Garnish with parsley and sprinkle with paprika.

MAKES 4 SERVINGS

CLASSIC VICHYSSOISE

4 medium leeks

4 medium potatoes

1 medium onion

1 garlic clove

3 tablespoons margarine or
    butter

4 cups chicken stock

1 cup heavy cream

1 cup milk

1 1/2 teaspoons salt

White pepper

2 tablespoons chopped
    fresh parsley

Wash leeks thoroughly. Trim the leeks to about 2 inches from the top of the bulb, discarding the coarse leaves. Cut leeks into thin slices. Peel potatoes and onion and cut into thin slices. Peel and mince garlic.

Melt the margarine or butter in a large kettle. Add the vegetables and sauté over medium heat for 4–5 minutes. Add chicken stock and simmer covered for about 15 minutes, or until vegetables are tender.

Purée mixture in a food processor or blender. Stir in the cream and milk. Chill. Season with salt and pepper. Taste and adjust seasoning if necessary. At serving time, garnish with parsley.

MAKES 8 SERVINGS

COCK-A-LEEKIE SOUP

*According to legend, this traditional Scottish soup
received its whimsical name during the days of cockfighting.
The loser was thrown into a kettle with leeks and
simmered into this classic soup.*

1 chicken, 3–4 pounds	6 medium leeks
2 quarts water	8 dried prunes (optional)
2¹/₂ teaspoons salt	2 tablespoons chopped fresh
¹/₄ teaspoon black pepper	parsley

Place chicken and water in a large kettle. Season with salt and pepper. Simmer covered for about 1 hour, or until tender. Skim fat from soup.

Wash leeks thoroughly. Trim the coarse leaves to about 2 inches from the top of the white portion. Slice the leeks lengthwise and rinse thoroughly. Cut leeks into 1-inch lengths. Add the leeks and prunes to the soup. Simmer covered for 20–30 minutes. Lift chicken from the soup. Remove the meat from the bones, discarding skin and bones. Dice chicken and return to soup, if desired. Taste, adding more seasoning, if necessary. Sprinkle with parsley right before serving.

MAKES 8 SERVINGS

VARIATION: Add 1 cup heavy cream to soup for Creamy Cock-a-Leekie.

CRAB-LEEK CRÊPES

Crêpes (recipe follows)
6 tablespoons margarine or
   butter, divided
1/4 cup flour
2 cups milk
1/2 teaspoon salt

Pinch of white pepper
6 medium leeks
8 ounces fresh or frozen
   crab meat
1/2 cup grated Gruyère
   cheese

Prepare crêpe batter several hours before preparing sauce.

Make white sauce: In a medium saucepan, melt 4 tablespoons margarine or butter. Stir in the flour and cook over medium heat for about 2 minutes. Gradually add milk. Bring to a boil, then reduce heat and simmer for about 10 minutes. Season with salt and pepper.

While sauce is simmering, prepare leeks. Wash the leeks and trim, discarding the green leaves. Split leeks into halves and chop into 1/2-inch pieces. In a medium skillet, melt remaining 2 tablespoons margarine or butter. Sauté leeks until tender. Add crab meat and keep warm.

Prepare the crêpes. Pour 1 cup white sauce into crab mixture. Spoon about 1/4 cup crab mixture on each crêpe and roll. Place crêpes seam side down in a lightly buttered baking dish, or lightly coated with a non stick cooking spray. Pour remaining sauce over crêpes. Top with cheese. Bake in preheated 350° F oven for 15 minutes. If desired, place under broiler for 2–3 minutes until lightly browned.

MAKES 4 SERVINGS, 2 CRÊPES EACH

CRÊPES

1 1/4 *cups flour*
Pinch of salt
2 *tablespoons margarine*
or butter

3 *eggs*
1 1/2 *cups milk*

In a blender or food processor, combine the flour and salt. Melt the margarine or butter. Add the margarine or butter, eggs, and milk to the flour mixture; blend well. Refrigerate the batter for a few hours or overnight.

To cook crêpes, use a well-seasoned 6- or 7-inch omelet or crêpe pan or an upside-down pan specially designed for crêpe cooking. If using a skillet, wipe it with an oiled paper towel. Heat the skillet until a drop of water sizzles on it. Remove from heat and pour 3 or 4 tablespoons batter into the skillet. Immediately twist the pan in a rolling motion to spread the batter. If there isn't enough batter to cover the bottom of the skillet, immediately add a little more. If too much, pour out the extra batter. Return the pan to the heat and cook for about 1 minute, or until the edges just start to curl and the bottom is golden brown. Turn the crêpe over with a spatula and cook for about 1 minute. Remove crêpe from the pan. Stack the crêpes with the second cooked side facing up. Brush the skillet with oil or melted butter in between cooking if a crêpe sticks to the pan.

If using an upside-down pan, dip it into the batter and turn upright immediately. When the edges start to curl, turn the crêpe over with a spatula and cook the other side. Stack the crêpes with the second cooked side facing up.

MAKES ABOUT 12 CRÊPES

LYCHEES AND LONGANS

These two aromatic and luscious fruits are members of the Sapindaceae *family and share many similar characteristics, making them interchangeable in recipes. The lychee, also known as litchi or lichee, of Oriental origin, and the longan, a native of India, have been popular Asian fruits since antiquity.*

A missionary serving in China is credited with introducing both fruits into the United States. China is a major producer of lychees, with other crops grown in other parts of Asia, Florida, Hawaii, Mexico, South America, Australia, and the Caribbean. The longan comes to U.S. markets chiefly from Hawaii, the Dominican Republic, and Florida.

Lychees are about 1–1¹/₂ inches in diameter and are covered with a thin, leathery shell ranging from bright red, orange red to reddish-brown or occasionally a coral color. Beneath the shell is a translucent, white, succulent fruit surrounding a smooth, brown seed. Lychees and longans have a flavor and texture similar to peeled grapes, but much more aromatic.

The longan, also known as lungan or "dragon's eyes," is about the same size as the lychee. It has a thin, brittle skin ranging in color from tannish-brown to yellowish-red. In comparison to the lychee, longans are less sweet and fragrant, with a more transparent but similar flesh also surrounding a shiny pit.

AVAILABILITY: Peak availability for lychees is June through July; longans are on the market July through August.

SELECTION AND STORAGE: Look for firm fruit with fresh, unbroken skin. The lychee's skin color darkens once harvested. Lychees and longans are ripe and ready to eat. Lychees will keep refrigerated in plastic for several weeks; longans are more perishable and won't keep as long. Both fruits freeze exceptionally well, just wrap unshelled fruit in a freezer bag and freeze up to 6 months.

PREPARATION: Both lychees and longans are easy to peel. Break open the shell at the stem end. Pull off the skin and remove the seed in the center of each fruit. These fruits are best when served chilled.

SERVING SUGGESTIONS:

- Add to fruit, poultry, or seafood salads.
- Drop fruit into champagne or sparkling wines.
- Toss into sweet-and-sour or stir-fried recipes.
- Drizzle fruit with orange-flavored liqueur and garnish with colorful, edible flowers.
- Serve fruit over frozen yogurt or ice cream.

NUTRITION INFORMATION: Both fruits are good sources of vitamin C and provide potassium and other nutrients. Longans have about 2 calories per fruit; lychees about 7 calories.

MINTED FRUIT AND CHICKEN SALAD

$^1/_3$ cup rice vinegar or cider
   vinegar
3 tablespoons olive oil
3 tablespoons chopped
   fresh mint
2 tablespoons honey
3 cups diced, cooked,
   and chilled chicken or
   turkey

$^3/_4$ pound lychees or longans
   (about 15)
2 medium peaches or
   nectarines
$^1/_2$ fresh pineapple
   Leaf lettuce or radicchio
   leaves
   Seedless red grape
   clusters
   Mint sprigs

In a cup, combine vinegar, oil, mint, and honey. Pour mixture over chicken. Cover and refrigerate 30 minutes.

Meanwhile prepare fruit. Shell lychees or longans; cut fruit away from seed. Thinly slice peaches or nectarines. Cut pineapple half lengthwise into halves; cut rind and core from each half, then cut crosswise into thin slices.

Line 4 dinner plates with lettuce or radicchio. Lift chicken from bowl with a slotted spoon and place in center. Arrange fruit around chicken. Drizzle some of the mint mixture over fruit. Garnish with grape clusters and mint sprigs.

MAKES 4 SERVINGS

GINGERED TROPICAL FRUIT SALAD

³/₄ pound fresh lychees or
   longans
2 kiwifruit
2 cups diced mango or
   papaya

1 large lime
1 (1¹/₂ inch) piece of fresh
   ginger
3 tablespoons honey

Shell lychees or longans; cut fruit from seed. Peel and slice kiwifruit, then cut slices into quarters. Combine lychees, kiwi, and mango or papaya in a serving dish.

Grate peel from lime. Squeeze juice and measure 2 tablespoons. Peel ginger; coarsely chop or slice ginger. Place ginger, lime juice, peel, and honey in a blender. Whirl until well-blended. Strain mixture through a fine-meshed sieve. Pour mixture over fruits and gently toss to coat.

MAKES 4 SERVINGS

RED, WHITE, AND BLUE FRUITS IN CHAMPAGNE

*Celebrate summer with some colorful seasonal fruits laced
in a ginger syrup and bubbly champagne.*

¹/₃ cup sugar
¹/₃ cup water
4 teaspoons chopped
   crystallized ginger
³/₄ pound fresh lychees or
   longans

1 cup fresh blueberries
12 small or medium
   strawberries
1 small bottle (187 ml) of
   champagne

In a medium saucepan, combine sugar, water, and ginger. Cook over medium heat until dissolved; bring to a boil and boil 1 minute. Remove from heat, transfer to a medium bowl; chill about 30 minutes.

Peel lychees or longans and cut fruit from the pit over the bowl of ginger syrup to catch all the juices. Cover and chill at least 1 hour or until serving time.

To serve, spoon lychees and syrup into 4 champagne or wine glasses. Divide blueberries among glasses and top with 3 strawberries. Pour in champagne and serve immediately.

MAKES 4 SERVINGS

MÂCHE

This tender, mild green has long been loved by Europeans. It is a salad green known by many names. Called "mâche" by the French, it is also known as "lamb's tongue" (perhaps due to the elongated leaf shape of some varieties), "lamb's lettuce," or "field salad" because it has been a pasture perennial since antiquity. The English refer to this green as "corn salad" because it grows easily alongside corn.

The leaves vary from round to somewhat elongated, are medium to dark green, and have a sweet flavor similar to Bibb lettuce.

AVAILABILITY: Year round.

SELECTION AND STORAGE: Mâche is generally sold in small bunches with the roots still attached. Look for fresh-looking greens. It is perishable so keep refrigerated and use promptly.

PREPARATION: Rinse very well. Trim off the root ends, swish several times in water, then pat dry.

SERVING SUGGESTIONS: Serve in simple salad creations. Nut oils and creamy dressings are particularly well-suited as dressing companions. Because the leaves are so tender, add the dressing right before serving. The interesting leaf shape also makes it good for using as a garnish.

NUTRITION INFORMATION: No nutrient data exists for mâche, but similar greens provide vitamins A and C, and are low in calories.

MÂCHE SALAD WITH HERBAL VINAIGRETTE

2 large tomatoes
6 scallions
1 large cucumber
¹/₄ cup minced fresh parsley

¹/₂ cup crumbled feta cheese
Herbal Vinaigrette
(recipe follows)
6 bunches mâche

Chop tomatoes. Bias-cut scallions into ¹/₂-inch pieces. Peel cucumber; remove seeds and dice. In a large bowl, combine tomato, scallions, cucumber, parsley, and feta cheese. Pour Herbal Vinaigrette over vegetables. Cover and chill at least 1 hour.

Rinse mâche well and drain. Gently separate mâche leaves at

base. Line outside edge of a large plate with mâche. Using a slotted spoon, mound vegetable mixture in center of mâche.

MAKES 4 SERVINGS

HERBAL VINAIGRETTE

2 tablespoons vegetable oil

2 tablespoons white wine vinegar

2 tablespoons water

1 tablespoon minced fresh oregano

2 teaspoons honey

1 teaspoon minced jalapeño pepper

Combine ingredients in a screw-top jar. Shake well to blend.

MÂCHE WITH RASPBERRY CREAM

A colorful spring salad bursting with fresh flavor!

2 bunches mâche (about 2 ounces)

1 head Boston or Bibb lettuce

2 teaspoons raspberry vinegar

1 teaspoon sugar

$1/8$ teaspoon salt

$2^1/2$ tablespoons heavy cream

$1^1/2$ tablespoons vegetable oil

2 ounces jícama

$1/2$ cup fresh raspberries

Gently separate mâche leaves at base. Separate lettuce leaves. Rinse, pat dry, and chill.

Combine vinegar, sugar, and salt in a small bowl. Whisk in cream; gradually add oil. Chill at least $1/2$ hour.

At serving time, line two salad plates with lettuce. Peel jícama; cut into thin julienne strips. Combine mâche and jícama and arrange over lettuce. Sprinkle with raspberries and drizzle with dressing.

MAKES 2 SERVINGS

$\mathcal{M}$AMEY SAPOTE

Underneath the mamey's (pronounced MAH-mey) leathery, coarse brown skin is a brilliantly colored, sweet and creamy flesh. Its smooth, avocadolike flesh ranges from pale salmon to pinkish or reddish-orange. The mamey has an exotic flavor reminiscent of pumpkin pudding with a touch of toasted almonds or spice, yet with its own alluring qualities. Shaped like a football, the mamey varies in size from 6 to 9 inches and ranges in weight from 1 to 4 pounds.

A native of Central and South America, the mamey sapote is a member of the Sapotaceae or Sapodilla family. Due to the cultivation of many sapodilla fruits in tropical countries around the world, there is a profusion of many colloquial names for fruits of this family and resulting confusion. For instance, the mamey sapote is not botanically related to another luscious tropical fruit, the white sapote (described on page 278).

The mamey is commercially cultivated in Florida and also grows in the Caribbean and from Mexico to South America.

AVAILABILITY: Mameys are rather limited in supply and are mainly available from January to April and June to October.

SELECTION AND STORAGE: Mameys must be ripe before use. Keep them at room temperature until they yield to a gentle squeeze. They can be refrigerated once ripe and should be used within a few days.

PREPARATION: The mamey's leathery skin is easily peeled, much the same as an avocado. The fruit can be sliced from the large, elliptical, shiny pit in the center.

SERVING SUGGESTIONS:

- Add slices to compotes and poultry or fruit salads.
- Accent its nutlike flavor with an almond or hazelnut liqueur.
- Purée for a fruit smoothie or use the purée for sauces or frozen desserts.
- Mash or purée for a vibrantly colored guacamole, sweeten if desired, and use as a dip for crisp-textured fruits or jícama.

NUTRITION INFORMATION: The mamey provides potassium, vitamins A and C, and other nutrients. A 1/2-cup contains about 100 calories.

SUNBURST MAMEY WITH BOURBON CREAM

Striking sunset-orange slices of mamey topped with bourbon cream is a fast and colorful finale to a meal.

2 egg yolks
1/3 cup sifted confectioners sugar
1 1/2 tablespoons bourbon
1/2 cup heavy cream

2 tablespoons slivered almonds
1 1/2 pound ripe mamey, chilled

In the top of a double boiler, beat egg yolks until lemon-colored. Beat in confectioners sugar. Gradually beat in the bourbon. Place over hot water and cook about 1 minute or until thickened, beating constantly.

Remove from heat and set top of double boiler in a large bowl of cracked ice. Beat mixture until it cools, about 1–2 minutes. In a separate bowl, whip the cream until stiff and fold into sauce. Pour into a covered container and chill.

Place almonds in a pie plate. Bake at 400° F about 3 minutes or until golden. Remove from oven; set aside.

At serving time, peel, pit, and thinly slice mamey. Arrange slices on 4 dessert plates in a sunburst pattern. Spoon some of the bourbon cream in the center of each plate. Garnish with toasted almonds.

MAKES 4 SERVINGS

MAMEY MOUSSE PIE

Pecan Crumb Crust
(recipe follows)
1 pint vanilla ice cream or
frozen yogurt, softened
1 cup mashed mamey pulp

1 1/4 cups heavy cream,
divided
1/2 cup confectioners sugar
1/2 teaspoon vanilla extract
Pecan halves for
garnish

Prepare Pecan Crumb Crust and cool. Spread ice cream or frozen yogurt in crust. Freeze until ice cream is firm.

Peel and cut mamey into chunks. Process in food processor until puréed. Combine 1 cup mamey pulp, 1/4 cup heavy cream, confectioners sugar, and vanilla in food processor; process until smooth. Transfer to a large bowl.

Beat remaining heavy cream until soft peaks form. Fold

whipped cream into mamey mixture. Spread on top of ice cream. Garnish with pecan halves. Freeze until set. Soften slightly in refrigerator before serving.

MAKES 8 SERVINGS

PECAN CRUMB CRUST

*½ cup finely chopped
  pecans
1 cup graham cracker
  crumbs*

*⅓ cup sugar
6 tablespoons margarine or
  butter, melted*

Mix the ingredients together; press firmly into a lightly buttered 9-inch pie plate. Bake at 350° F for 10–15 minutes or until lightly browned. Cool.

MAMEY WITH RUM-BUTTER SAUCE

*3 tablespoons butter
½ cup sifted confectioners
  sugar
1 egg yolk, beaten
1½ tablespoons rum*

*¼ cup heavy cream
1½ tablespoons chopped
  pecans or hazelnuts
1½ pounds mamey
  Sweetened whipped
  cream*

In top of a double boiler, combine 3 tablespoons melted butter, confectioners sugar, egg yolk, and rum; mix well. Gradually stir in cream. Place top of double boiler over boiling water and cook over medium-high heat about 5–6 minutes or until mixture is slightly thickened. Remove from heat; set aside.

Place nuts on a pie plate. Bake in a preheated 400° F oven about 3 minutes or until toasted.

Peel, pit, and cut mamey into thin slices. Arrange slices on 4 individual dessert plates, with the ends radiating from the top of the plate. Drizzle about 2 tablespoons sauce over slices. Place a small dollop of whipped cream at the point where the slices meet and sprinkle with a few nuts.

MAKES 4 SERVINGS

HOT GINGER TURKEY WITH MAMEY ON SALAD GREENS

Substitute about 1 pound of peeled and sliced mamey for the white sapote in the recipe on page 281. Reduce orange juice to 3 tablespoons; moistening slices with additional orange juice isn't necessary to prevent darkening.

MANGO

The mango is a familiar fruit around the globe, better known than apples in more than half of the world! This luscious tropical fruit has a rich, alluring flavor that is delicately fragrant when ripe and exceptionally juicy.

The mango has been cultivated for perhaps 6,000 years and originated near India and/or Malayasia. In the sixteenth century, mangos were introduced into South Africa and Brazil by the Portuguese and later into Florida. Today commercial varieties available in the U.S. are grown in the Caribbean, Florida, Mexico, and Central America. Asia is a leading producer of this tropical favorite for markets around the world.

The mango's flesh is juicy, yellow or golden orange, and can be either smooth or fibrous. A ripe mango is exquisite in flavor—some liken it to a combination of a peach or nectarine with a hint of pineapple and a splash of citrus overtones. Ripeness is especially critical for this fruit—an unripe mango jolts the senses; it is acid, bitter, and smacks of turpentine. Mangos must be fully ripe to achieve their finest flavor.

Mango can be oval, round, or kidney-shaped. Most commercial varieties weigh 1/2–2 pounds with the average about 1 pound. The skin color of ripe mangos ranges from green-yellow to orange and crimson. Some varieties change color as they ripen while others do not, so skin color is not a reliable indicator of ripeness.

Mangos are not frequently marketed by variety, but the following varieties are some of those most available to U.S. consumers.

- *Francescae, Francis, Francisque* is all green with an S-curve shape.
- *Haden* can be either round, slightly oval, or kidney-shaped and generally weighs less than a pound. The skin changes from green to yellowish-orange as it ripens and acquires a distinctive rosy blush.

- *Keitt* is a large, round fruit that can weigh several pounds. It remains green when ripe with a subtle orange or rose blush. The flesh is nearly fiberless, juicy, and sweet.
- *Kent* is oval to round, weighing on average a little more than 1 pound. When ripe, the skin is orangish-yellow, speckled with green and blushed with crimson. Its flesh is smooth, sweet with a touch of lime.
- *Tommy Atkins* is oval and weighs about 1 pound with a thick, orange or yellow skin which is speckled or blushed.
- *Van Dyke* is oval and generally about 10 ounces in weight. The skin of this variety when ripe can be yellow or reddish-orange. The flesh is orange and a bit fibrous with a flavor reminiscent of pineapple.

AVAILABILITY: January through the fall, with peak supplies during the summer months.

SELECTION AND STORAGE: Since there are so many differences in characteristics among mango varieties, choose fresh-looking fruit with firm skin. Skin color is not a reliable sign of ripeness since not all varieties change color as they ripen. Aroma is a good indicator of ripeness. A ripe mango has a fragrant aroma at the stem end. A lack of fragrance usually indicates the fruit has little flavor.

To ripen, keep mangos at room temperature until fragrant and tender. Some varieties when ripe will yield to gentle pressure yet remain firm, while others become very soft. Once ripe, mangos can be refrigerated. Use ripe fruit within a few days for maximum flavor.

PREPARATION: Mangos can be peeled easily by scoring the skin in quarters from the top to the stem end, then peeling like a banana. Smaller mangos can be peeled and eaten out of hand. For slicing, score the fruit as above and then cut the fruit from the pit. The fruit clings to the elliptically shaped pit, so slice as much of the flesh from the pit as possible.

SERVING SUGGESTIONS:

- Serve chunks in poultry, tossed, or fruit salads.
- Top pancakes, waffles, or French toast with diced mango, or use as a filling for crêpes.
- Add mango slices or chunks to seafood, meat, or poultry stir-fry recipes.
- Drizzle slices with orange liqueur and serve as a dessert or over angel food cake or ice cream.
- Purée fruit for sherbets, ices, or parfaits.
- In the tropics, green, immature mangos are used in chutneys, relishes, and pickles.

NUTRITION INFORMATION: Mangos are an excellent source of vitamins A and C, provide potassium, and are low in sodium. One medium fruit has about 135 calories.

PARADISE SALAD

1 mango, about 1 pound
1 large papaya
2 cups watermelon balls
1/2 cup shredded coconut

1/4 cup slivered almonds
1/4 cup vanilla yogurt
1 tablespoon honey

Peel, seed, and dice the mango and papaya. Combine fruits and coconut in a salad bowl. Toast the almonds in a small, nonstick skillet until golden; add to the fruits. Mix together yogurt and honey and pour over salad ingredients. Toss to coat. Garnish with toasted almonds.

MAKES 4 TO 6 SERVINGS

CREAMY CARDAMOM FRUIT SALAD

1 mango, about 1 pound
2 cups honeydew melon balls
1 cup halved and seeded red
  grapes
1 cup sliced fresh strawberries
3 ounces cream cheese,
  softened

2 tablespoons fresh lemon
  or lime juice
2 tablespoons honey
2 tablespoons milk
1/2 teaspoon ground
  cardamom

Peel, pit, and dice the mango. In a medium serving bowl, combine fruits and chill. In a small mixing bowl, combine cream cheese, lemon or lime juice, and honey. Using an electric mixer, beat mixture at low speed until smooth and creamy. Add milk and cardamom and continue beating until smooth. Pour dressing over fruits and toss to coat.

MAKES 4 SERVINGS

MANGO-PEACH BETTY

2 mangos, each about 1
  pound
3 medium peaches
1 tablespoon fresh lemon or
  lime juice
2/3 cup all-purpose flour

1/2 cup firmly packed
  brown sugar
4 tablespoons margarine
  or butter, softened
1 1/2 teaspoons ground
  cinnamon

Peel, pit, and dice fruits. Place in a 9-inch pie plate. Sprinkle fruits with lemon or lime juice. In a medium bowl, combine flour, brown sugar, margarine or butter, and cinnamon, mixing until crumbly. Sprinkle brown sugar mixture over fruit. Bake in pre-heated 375° F oven for 25–30 minutes. Serve warm or cold with ice cream, whipped cream, or frozen yogurt.

MAKES 6 SERVINGS

MANGO TORTONI

2 eggs, separated
1/2 cup sifted confectioners
   sugar
1 teaspoon vanilla extract

1 cup heavy cream
1 mango, about 1 pound
1 cup shortbread cookie
   crumbs, divided

In a small bowl, beat the egg whites until stiff; set aside. In a medium bowl, combine the egg yolks, confectioners sugar, and vanilla, beating well. Fold beaten egg whites into the yolk mixture. In a separate bowl, whip the cream until stiff.

Peel, pit, and finely chop the mango; measure 1 cup chopped mango. Fold the whipped cream, mango, and 1/2 cup cookie crumbs into the egg mixture. Spoon the mixture into a buttered 8-inch-square pan. Sprinkle remaining crumbs on top. Freeze until firm. Remove from freezer about 20 minutes before serving. Cut into squares.

MAKES 6 SERVINGS

MANGO TRIFLE

A delicious blending of flavors and textures.

5 tablespoons sugar,
   divided
¹/₄ cup cornstarch
1¹/₃ cups milk
3 eggs
2 teaspoons vanilla
   extract, divided
12 ladyfingers

¹/₃ cup raspberry jam
¹/₄ cup light rum
2 mangos, each about 1
   pound
1 tablespoon fresh lemon or
   lime juice
1 cup heavy cream
   Fresh berries for garnish

In the top of a double boiler, combine 4 tablespoons sugar and the cornstarch; gradually add milk, blending well. Cook over boiling water until sauce is thickened, stirring frequently. Beat eggs and add to mixture, stirring until well-blended and thickened. Remove from heat; add 1¹/₂ teaspoons vanilla. Chill uncovered for about 1 hour.

Split ladyfingers and place in a 2¹/₂-quart serving dish or glass bowl. Spread a thin layer of jam over ladyfingers. Drizzle rum over ladyfingers. Peel, pit, and dice the mangos. Sprinkle lemon or lime juice over fruit. Layer fruit on ladyfingers. Whip the cream. Combine half of the whipped cream with the chilled custard. Spoon over fruit. Add 1 tablespoon sugar and ¹/₂ teaspoon vanilla to remaining cream. Spread whipped cream over the top; garnish with berries and serve.

MAKES 8 SERVINGS

MANGO ICE CREAM PIE

Graham Cracker Crust
(see page 242)
2 mangos, each about 1
  pound

1 1/2 cups vanilla ice cream,
  slightly softened
1/4 cup light rum
1/2 cup sliced almonds

Prepare the Graham Cracker Crust and set aside. Peel, pit, and coarsely chop the mangos. Purée the mangos in a blender or food processor; measure 1 1/2 cups purée. In a large bowl, combine mango purée and ice cream. Stir in the rum. Spoon the mixture into the prepared crust. Toast the almonds and sprinkle over the pie. Freeze until firm. Remove the pie from the freezer about 15 minutes before serving. Drizzle with a little chilled Mango-Rum Sauce (see recipe on page 171), if desired.

MAKES 6 TO 8 SERVINGS

MICROWAVE MANGO CHUTNEY GLAZE

*Use as a glaze for poultry or pork during the last few
minutes of grilling or serve as a condiment.*

1 mango, about 1 pound
1 1/2 tablespoons raisins
2 tablespoons sugar
2 tablespoons cider
  vinegar

1 teaspoon minced fresh
  gingerroot
1 garlic clove, minced
1/4 teaspoon salt

Peel mango and cut flesh from the pit. Place in a food processor with the remaining ingredients and process just until mango is puréed (raisins will purée easily after cooking). Transfer mango mixture to a 1-quart microwaveable bowl. Cover and cook on full power 2–3 minutes; stir and cook 1–2 minutes longer or until the mixture thickens and becomes slightly transparent. Return mixture to food processor; purée until smooth. If mixture thickens too much, add a little water to the mixture and stir well.

MAKES ABOUT ³/₄ CUP

VARIATION: Add 1 teaspoon chili pepper or more to taste before puréeing.

NOTE: This recipe easily doubles. Increase cooking time to a total of about 6–7 minutes, stirring halfway through cooking.

MANGO-RUM SAUCE

Luscious served warm or chilled over angel food, chiffon, or pound cake, ice cream or frozen yogurt. Try it as a topping for waffles or pancakes, too.

2 mangos, each about 1 pound
¹/₂ cup sugar
¹/₂ cup freshly squeezed orange juice

1 tablespoons fresh lime juice
4 teaspoons cornstarch
2 tablespoons rum

Peel, pit, and dice the mangos. In a medium saucepan, combine diced mango, sugar, juices, and cornstarch. Bring mixture to a boil over medium-high heat; boil 1–2 minutes or until thickened. Remove from heat; stir in rum. Serve warm or chilled.

MAKES 2 CUPS

MACADAMIA NUT AND MANGO CHICKEN

1¹/₂ pounds boneless chicken breast
1 teaspoon minced fresh ginger
2 tablespoons cornstarch, divided
2 tablespoons sherry, divided
4 tablespoons peanut oil, divided
2 tablespoons reduced-sodium soy sauce

2 tablespoons sugar
1 tablespoon white wine vinegar
¹/₄ cup chicken stock or broth
¹/₂ pound Chinese cabbage
1 medium red pepper
1 mango, about 1 pound
4 scallions
¹/₂ cup coarsely chopped macadamia nuts
Hot cooked rice

Remove skin from chicken; cut into thin strips. Place chicken in a dish. Combine ginger, 1 tablespoon each of the cornstarch, sherry, and oil. Pour mixture over chicken and toss to coat; allow to marinate while preparing other ingredients.

In a cup, combine remaining 1 tablespoon of the cornstarch and sherry, soy sauce, sugar, vinegar, and chicken stock; stir to blend. Set aside.

Shred the cabbage and measure 3 cups. Remove seeds and membrane from pepper; cut into 1-inch pieces. Peel, pit, and dice mango. Slice scallions into 1-inch lengths.

In a large skillet or wok, heat 1 tablespoon oil. Add the nuts and stir-fry just until golden. Remove nuts and drain on paper towels.

Heat remaining 2 tablespoons oil. Add chicken and stir-fry about 3–4 minutes or until chicken is done. Remove chicken with a slotted spoon. Set aside.

Add cabbage and red pepper; stir-fry 2 minutes. Return

chicken to skillet; add mango and reserved sauce. Stir until mixture thickens. Stir in scallions. Transfer to serving dish. Sprinkle with macadamia nuts. Serve over rice.

MAKES 4 SERVINGS

SPECIALTY MUSHROOMS

Mushroom lovers can rejoice in the ever-expanding specialty varieties now available for adding exotic interest to recipes. There are about 2,000 species of mushrooms eaten around the world; however, only a fraction are commercially available. Mushroom cultivation is exacting, and technological advances now enable greater domestication of some of these varieties.

CÊPE
(Porcini, Bolete, Cep)

This full-bodied, pungent mushroom, highly regarded by those who have been captivated by its sumptuous, meaty, melting texture, is unfortunately rather limited in availability. It resembles a cultivated mushroom with a bulbous, light-colored stem topped with a tan to brownish cap, 1–10 inches in diameter. Underneath the cap is a spongy mass of holes or tubes, rather than gills.

SELECTION AND STORAGE: Generally, the best specimens have caps 6–7 inches in diameter with pale undersides. These mushrooms absorb other aromas and likewise lose their own flavor quickly, so do not store them long. Refrigerate covered with a damp towel and plan to use them promptly.

PREPARATION: Select simple recipes for featuring these glorious mushroom treasures. To prepare, brush or trim the base. The stems are tasty and tender (although a bit more fibrous) so be sure to use these along with the caps. Check under the caps—trim away any bitter yellowish, brownish, or slimy parts.

CHANTRELLES
(Trumpet mushroom)

Long a European favorite, the distinctively shaped chantrelle mushroom has many variations in color and shape. Resembling a trumpet, funnel, or inverted umbrella, some have gill-like ridges on the caps while other species have none at all. Chantrelles can be white, pale yellow, apricot, reddish-orange, dark brown, black, or even deep purple.

Chantrelles have an enticing aroma similar to apricots with a flavor hinting of champagne, almonds, or cinnamon.

AVAILABILITY: Erratic availability from summer through winter.

SELECTION AND STORAGE: Chantrelles should be plump with a firm, spongy texture. Store covered in a single layer covered with a lightly dampened paper towel or cheesecloth. Use within 1 week.

PREPARATION: It is best to brush mushrooms gently or wipe them with a damp cloth to clean. However, chantrelles may need to be rinsed and blotted dry. Trim off heavy bases. If small, leave them whole, larger ones can be cut into bite-size pieces.

CREMINI OR ROMAN MUSHROOMS

Cremini mushrooms have a bolder flavor than the more familiar cultivated Agaricus bisporous variety. They can be handled and prepared in the same way.

AVAILABILITY: Year round.

SELECTION AND STORAGE: The freshest mushrooms are closed around the stem by a sheath or veil. Those having open veils, caused by a loss of moisture as they mature, are fine to use, but should be used promptly. Store either in the refrigerator in a paper (not plastic) bag or in the cardboard or plastic container in which they were purchased. Mushrooms purchased with their veils intact can be refrigerated in good condition up to one week.

PREPARATION: Wipe mushrooms with a damp cloth. Avoid scrubbing or peeling them. Slice off a thin portion from the stem. Use raw or cooked as the common mushroom.

ENOKI
(Enoikdake, Enokitake, Golden Mushroom, Velvet Stem)

These delicate, white, tiny-capped mushrooms with their long stems are graceful, elegant-looking members of the mushroom family. The enoki, a delicacy in Japan, has a mild, sweet flavor with a slightly crunchy texture. Their crisp texture makes them an ideal salad or sandwich ingredient, and their naturally graceful design make them a striking garnish. Use much as you might raw bean sprouts. Enokis are best eaten raw rather than cooked.

AVAILABILITY: Year round.

SELECTION AND STORAGE: Currently, enoki mushrooms are marketed in plastic packets. Look for packages with mushrooms which are firm, white to creamy-white in color. The spongy bases should not be watery or discolored. At home, store the packets in the refrigerator and use within a few days.

PREPARATION: Simply rinse and trim off the spongy cluster at the base of the stems, along with 1–2 inches of the stems. Separate the stems and use, as desired.

MOREL

Morels have a rich, earthy flavor and have honeycomb, cone-shaped caps. They can be tan, dark brown, or yellow, and they range in size.

AVAILABILITY: Early spring through July.

SELECTION AND STORAGE: Select those with dry, spongy caps. Morels should have an earthy aroma reminiscent of hazelnuts. At home, store them in a single layer, covered with a paper towel or cheesecloth. If caps are exceptionally dry, cover mushrooms with a moistened paper towel. Use within a few days.

PREPARATION: Trim off the heavy tips of the base, slicing off any tough stems. Small morels can be kept whole; larger ones can be cut. When cut crosswise, they resemble little wreaths. Their convoluted caps may require rinsing to remove clinging soil. Blot dry and use immediately. Morels must be cooked. *Never eat them raw.*

OYSTER

This tender, delicate-tasting cultivated mushroom has a chamoislike, fan-shaped cap with deep gills. Their short stems are joined in a cluster at the base. Oyster mushrooms vary in size depending on the particular strain.

AVAILABILITY: Year round.

SELECTION AND STORAGE: Look for dry, evenly colored mushrooms with silky, suedelike caps. They are perishable, so use them promptly. At home keep mushrooms refrigerated, wrapped in damp, paper towels, and use as soon as possible.

PREPARATION: These are very clean mushrooms and generally only require a bit of brushing. Cut off the tips of the stems. Large caps can be cut into pieces, while smaller mushrooms can be kept whole. Use oyster mushrooms in simple dishes to best appreciate their delicate flavor.

SHIITAKE
(Oriental Black Mushroom, Chinese Black Mushroom)

Once only cultivated in the Orient, these large, parasol-shaped mushrooms are becoming more widely available. Their fleshy texture and rich, exotic, woodsy flavor is enchanting. Shiitakes have long been appreciated in Oriental dishes, but they boldly transform everyday dishes as well.

AVAILABILITY: Year round.

SELECTION AND STORAGE: Look for plump, firm mushrooms with thick, dry caps ranging in color from gold to dark brown. Shiitakes do not have a veil or covering between the stem and cap. If not pre-packaged, check for a distinctive aroma. Refrigerate at home and, if purchased in good condition, they should keep a week or more.

PREPARATION: Trim the bases and clean the caps with a damp paper towel. The stems are a little tougher than the common mushroom, so they should be thinly sliced or chopped. Shiitakes can be prepared in the same ways as the common cultivated mushroom.

NUTRITION INFORMATION: Although nutritional values vary according to the variety, fresh mushrooms provide potassium, some protein, and other nutrients. A $1/2$-cup serving is sodium-free and has just nine calories.

MUSHROOM CROUSTADES

Toasted bread cups cradle a creamy mushroom and
scallion filling for an extraordinary appetizer.

CROUSTADES

1 tablespoon margarine or butter	*18 slices white bread*

MUSHROOM FILLING

½ pound fresh mushrooms
(chanterelle, oyster, or
shiitake)
2 scallions
4 tablespoons margarine or
butter
2 tablespoons all-purpose
flour

1 cup heavy cream
2 tablespoons chopped
fresh parsley
2 teaspoons fresh lemon
juice
¼ teaspoon salt
Grated Parmesan cheese

Prepare croustades. Melt the margarine or butter and brush inside of 18 muffin cups with it. Cut out a 3-inch circle from each slice of bread. Press circles into tins. Bake in preheated 375° F oven for about 10 minutes or until golden. Remove and set aside.

To prepare the filling, clean mushrooms and chop them. Thinly slice scallions; set aside.

In a large skillet, melt the margarine or butter. Add the mushrooms and sauté 3 minutes over medium heat. Sprinkle flour over mushrooms. Gradually stir in the cream and cook about 2 minutes until the mixture thickens. Remove from heat. Stir in scallions, parsley, lemon juice, and salt.

Place croustades on a baking sheet. Fill each croustade with some of the mushroom mixture. Sprinkle a little Parmesan cheese over each croustade. Bake at 375° F for 8–10 minutes or until cheese is golden.

MAKES 18 APPETIZERS

NOTE: Croustades can be prepared in advance and refrigerated. Allow extra time for reheating.

ORIENTAL SALAD WITH SESAME VINAIGRETTE AND WON TON CRISPS

8 won ton wrappers
  Peanut oil
1/4 pound fresh snow peas
1 package (3–3 1/2 ounces)
  enoki mushrooms
3 scallions

1 medium red bell pepper
3 cups thinly sliced Chinese
  cabbage or red cabbage
  Sesame Vinaigrette (recipe
  follows)

SESAME VINAIGRETTE

2 tablespoons wine vinegar
2 teaspoons reduced-sodium
  soy sauce

1/4 cup peanut oil
1/2 teaspoon sugar
1/2 teaspoon sesame oil

Preheat oven to 350° F. Cut won ton wrappers into 1/2-inch strips. Place on a lightly oiled baking sheet. Brush strips with a little peanut oil. Bake about 3–4 minutes or until lightly browned and crisp. Remove from oven and set aside.

Rinse and trim snow peas; cut snow peas in half. Plunge snow peas into boiling water and cook for 1 minute. Drain and plunge snow peas into ice water. Allow to chill in ice water while preparing other vegetables.

Trim about 1–2 inches from the bottom of the mushrooms; rinse and pat dry. Thinly slice scallions. Seed and remove membrane from pepper; cut pepper into thin strips about 2–3 inches.

Drain snow peas and pat dry. In a large bowl, combine cabbage with snow peas, enoki mushrooms, scallions, and bell pepper.

In a small bowl or cup, combine ingredients for Sesame Vinaigrette. Pour Sesame Vinaigrette over salad, toss to coat thoroughly. Garnish with won ton crisps.

MAKES 4 SERVINGS

SHIITAKE MUSHROOM AND PORK SOUP

1/4 pound fresh shiitake mushrooms
1/2 pound boneless pork Coarsely ground black pepper
2 tablespoons peanut oil
1 garlic clove, minced

4 cups chicken broth
2 teaspoons reduced-sodium soy sauce
2 tablespoons white or cider vinegar
3 scallions, thinly sliced

Wipe mushrooms with a damp cloth. Trim stems and thinly slice the stems and caps (you should have about 1 1/2 cups sliced mushrooms).

Trim any fat from the pork; cut meat into thin, bite-size strips. Season pork with pepper. Heat oil in a large saucepan. Add the pork and garlic; sauté just until pork changes color. Add the mushrooms; sauté for 1 more minute.

Stir in the broth and soy sauce; bring to a boil. Stir in vinegar, cook 1 or 2 minutes longer. Ladle into a soup tureen or individual bowls. Garnish with scallions.

MAKES 4 TO 5 SERVINGS

SNAP BEAN AND SHIITAKE SAUTÉ

*3/4 pound fresh green or wax
beans*
*1/4 pound fresh shiitake
mushrooms*
*4 teaspoons bottled oyster
sauce*
2 teaspoons honey

2 teaspoons water
*2 teaspoons sesame seeds,
toasted*
1 tablespoon peanut oil
*1 tablespoon margarine or
butter*

Wash and trim beans. Thinly slice mushroom caps and stems. Set vegetables aside. In a cup, combine oyster sauce, honey, and water. In a medium, nonstick skillet, toast sesame seeds. Remove from skillet; set aside.

In the same skillet, heat oil. Add beans and cook 2 minutes over medium-high heat, stirring constantly. Add mushrooms; cook 2 minutes more or until beans are crisp-tender. Pour reserved oyster sauce–honey mixture over vegetables and toss to coat thoroughly. Transfer to a serving dish. Sprinkle with toasted sesame seeds.

MAKES 4 SERVINGS

OYSTER MUSHROOMS AND PORK MEDALLIONS IN DIJON-WINE SAUCE

*1/2 pound fresh oyster
mushrooms
1 1/4 pounds pork tenderloin
Coarsely ground black
pepper
4 tablespoons margarine
or butter, divided
3 garlic cloves, minced
1 teaspoon cornstarch*

*2 teaspoons Dijon mustard
2 teaspoons Worcestershire
sauce
1/4 cup dry white wine
1/4 cup chicken stock
1 tablespoon minced fresh
parsley*

Wipe mushrooms with damp cloth; trim stem ends and separate mushrooms from clusters. Thinly slice thick stems. Coarsely chop large mushrooms; set aside.

Cut tenderloin into 1-inch thick slices; flatten with a mallet. Season medallions with pepper. In a large, nonstick skillet, melt 2 tablespoons margarine or butter. Add garlic and medallions; cook over medium heat about 8–10 minutes or until done, turning medallions occasionally while cooking. Meanwhile in a cup, combine cornstarch, mustard, and Worcestershire sauce, stirring until well-blended. Gradually stir in wine and chicken stock; set aside.

Place medallions on a serving platter; keep warm. In the same skillet, melt remaining 2 tablespoons margarine or butter. Add mushrooms and sauté about 2 minutes or until tender. Pour wine mixture into skillet, stirring just until thickened. Spoon mushrooms and sauce over medallions. Sprinkle with parsley.

MAKES 4 SERVINGS

VEAL SCALOPPINI WITH CHANTERELLES

1/2 pound fresh chanterelles*
2 teaspoons flour
1/2 cup chicken stock or
　broth
2 tablespoons marsala wine
1 tablespoon lemon juice
1/2 pound veal scaloppini

Flour
Salt and pepper
2 garlic cloves
5 tablespoons margarine or
　butter, divided
1 tablespoon minced fresh
　parsley

Wipe mushrooms with a damp cloth, or if necessary quickly toss in a strainer under running water and blot dry. Cut caps into bite-size pieces. Trim heavy tips off bases and discard. Set mushrooms aside.

In a measuring cup, add 2 teaspoons flour. Pour in a little chicken stock or broth and stir until smooth. Add remaining stock, wine, and lemon juice; set aside.

Pound the veal with a meat mallet. Dredge with flour seasoned with salt and pepper. Peel and mince the garlic; set aside.

In a medium skillet, melt 2 tablespoons margarine or butter. Add mushrooms and sauté over medium heat for 2–3 minutes or until tender. Remove from skillet.

In the same skillet, melt remaining 3 tablespoons margarine or butter. Add the garlic and veal; sauté over medium-high heat for about 4 minutes or until done, browning on both sides. Add mushrooms, reserved stock mixture, and parsley; cook about 1 minute or until sauce thickens.

Place veal on serving plate; spoon sauce and mushrooms over scaloppini.

MAKES 2 SERVINGS

*If chanterelles aren't available, substitute another mushroom.

PAPAYA

Of tropical origin, the smooth, mellow papaya offers a fresh taste of paradise. Its flavor is both fruity and fragrant and it resembles a melon in texture. In fact, the papaya, which grows in clusters on trees, is known as the "tree melon."

The Spaniards discovered the papaya in tropical America during the sixteenth century. This tropical treasure was later introduced into the Philippines, Africa, and Asia. Now papayas are grown in tropical and subtropical regions around the world.

Worldwide, there are different varieties of papaya ranging in size, shape, and color. The Solo variety is pear-shaped. The Kapoho Solo is yellow-fleshed; the Sunrise Solo from Hawaii and the Caribbean Sunrise from the Bahamas is salmon or rose-fleshed. The Solo varieties generally weigh about 1 pound. Other larger varieties, some weighing 10 or more pounds, are grown in Mexico, the Philippines, the Caribbean, and other tropical regions. Larger varieties are often sold in wedges.

The papaya's center is filled with grayish-black seeds resembling caviar. The seeds are edible and can be ground to the size of coarse pepper and used in dressings or meat marinades.

Papayas, particularly when they're green, contain a natural enzyme, papain, which breaks down protein, making it a useful meat tenderizer. To use papaya in this way, pierce meat with a fork and spread mashed papaya pulp over meat.

AVAILABILITY: Papayas are available year round, with peak availability May through November.

SELECTION AND STORAGE: In the produce department, papayas are marketed in varying stages of ripeness ranging from fully green to golden yellow. Papayas should ripen at room temperature until they yield to gentle palm pressure. The skin color of Solo varieties turn from green to golden as they ripen; Mexican varieties retain much of their green skin color when ripe.

Once ripe, papayas can be refrigerated. Use ripe papayas within a few days.

PREPARATION: Cut the fruit lengthwise into halves, scoop out the seeds, squeeze fresh lemon or lime juice over the fruit, and scoop out the fruit with a spoon. For other uses, peel the skin using a peeler or paring knife, discard the seeds, and cut as desired.

SERVING SUGGESTIONS:

- Add chunks to fruit, tossed, poultry, or ham salads.
- Combine chunks of papaya, celery, and pineapple with red grapes and shrimp. Toss with mayonnaise flavored with curry and lemon or lime juice. Spoon mixture into hollowed papaya halves.
- Cut fruit into halves and scoop out seeds. Fill centers with a scoop of vanilla or fruit ice cream, sherbet, or frozen yogurt.

- Cut off 1 1/2 inches from the top of the papaya. Scoop out seeds and fill fruit with poultry, seafood, or ham salad. Chill, then slice crosswise into rounds.
- Make a daiquiri with puréed papaya, lime juice, rum, and sugar.
- Wrap thinly sliced prosciutto around slices of papaya.
- Sprinkle slices with sugar and lime and sauté briefly. Serve as an accompaniment to poultry, seafood, or meat dishes.
- Cooks from regions familiar with the papaya's versatility also use the papaya green and unripe. When cooked, unripe papaya resembles squash in flavor. Another frequent use of green papaya is for marinating or pickling.

NUTRITION INFORMATION: Papayas are an excellent source of vitamins A and C. An average half (Solo variety) has about 60 calories and is low in sodium.

CHILLED PAPAYA SOUP

A sparkling appetizer soup with a taste of paradise.

2 papayas
3/4 cup fresh orange juice
1/4 cup fresh lime juice
1/4 cup honey

1 cup dry white wine
1 cup club soda
Sliced fresh strawberries

Peel, seed, and coarsely chop the papayas. In a food processor or blender, purée the papayas. Combine orange juice, lime juice, and honey with purée; blend well. Add wine and blend. Chill mixture. To serve, add club soda and garnish with a few sliced strawberries.

MAKES 1 QUART

TROPICAL FRUIT AND LAMB KEBOBS

2 pounds boneless lamb	2 teaspoons curry powder
1 medium onion	1 teaspoon salt
2 garlic cloves	1/4 teaspoon black pepper
1 tablespoon vegetable oil	2 medium bananas
1 large papaya	12 large chunks of fresh
2 tablespoons brown sugar	pineapple
2 tablespoons white vinegar	

Trim lamb of fat, cut into 1½-inch cubes, and place in a medium mixing bowl. Peel and chop the onion and garlic.

Heat the oil in a medium skillet. Sauté the onion and garlic until tender. Cut the papaya into halves and discard the seeds. Mash half of the papaya with a fork. Peel the other half and cut into 1½-inch cubes; set aside. Add mashed papaya, brown sugar, vinegar, curry, and seasonings to onion and garlic, mixing to blend. Pour mixture over lamb. Cover and refrigerate for at least 4 hours, or more.

Peel the bananas and cut into 1-inch chunks. Thread meat alternately with reserved papaya, bananas, and pineapple on skewers. Grill over hot coals, turning occasionally, until done.

MAKES 4 SERVINGS

PAPAYA BRUNCH PUFF

A fluffy pancake omelet is topped with sliced papaya and dusted with confectioners sugar.

2 eggs
2/3 cup flour
2/3 cup milk
1 tablespoon margarine or butter

2 large papayas
Sifted confectioners sugar

Beat eggs, flour, and milk together until smooth. Place a 10-inch ovenproof skillet* in a preheated 450° F oven for about 3 minutes, or until the skillet is very hot. Remove skillet from oven, add margarine or butter, and allow to melt. Pour batter into skillet. Bake at 450° F for 10 minutes, then reduce temperature to 350° F and bake for 10–15 minutes longer, until puffy and lightly golden. While puff is baking, peel, seed, and dice papayas.

Place puff on a serving platter. Fill puff with diced papaya and sprinkle with confectioners sugar. Serve immediately.

MAKES 4 SERVINGS

* If using a skillet without an ovenproof handle, cover handle completely with several thicknesses of aluminum foil.

PARADISE SHRIMP SALAD

1/2 pound medium shrimp
2 papayas
1/3 cup chili sauce
3 tablespoons fresh lemon or lime juice

1 tablespoon vegetable oil
Black pepper
1/4 cup chopped watercress

Cook shrimp in boiling water for about 2–3 minutes, or until they turn pink and are cooked through; drain. Remove the shells and devein the shrimp; Chill. Cut papayas into halves and scoop out the seeds. Gently remove papaya flesh from the shells and dice. Reserve papaya shells. Place diced papaya and chilled shrimp in a medium bowl.

In a screw-top jar, combine the chili sauce, lemon or lime juice, oil, and black pepper to taste. Add the watercress and blend well. Pour the dressing over the papaya-shrimp mixture and toss to coat. Spoon the mixture into the papaya shells and serve.

MAKES 4 SERVINGS

TROPICAL LUNCHEON SALAD

Fresh snow peas, papaya, ham, and strawberries are drizzled with a tangy fruit dressing.

$1/4$ *pound fresh snow peas*	2 *tablespoons white wine*
2 *papayas*	*vinegar*
1 *pint fresh strawberries*	2 *tablespoons fresh lime juice*
$1/4$ *pound ham*	3 *tablespoons vegetable oil*
	Leaf lettuce

Trim snow peas and place in boiling water for 1 minute; drain, then plunge peas into ice water until well-chilled. Drain.

Cut papayas into halves and remove seeds. Scoop into balls and place balls in a mixing bowl. Wash and hull strawberries. Reserve 5 medium berries and set aside. Slice remaining berries and place in the mixing bowl. Cut snow peas into halves. Slice ham into julienne strips. Add snow peas and ham to mixing bowl. In a small bowl, mash reserved berries. Add vinegar, lime juice, and oil to mashed berries, mixing well. Pour dressing over salad mixture and toss to coat. Place on lettuce-lined salad plates and serve.

MAKES 4 SERVINGS

ISLAND BREEZE PIE

This glamorous dessert is a snap to make. A refreshing combination of ice cream and sherbet is swirled into a gingersnap crust, then topped with a colorful combination of fresh fruits laced with liqueur.

1²/₃ cups gingersnap cookie crumbs	1 papaya
4 tablespoons margarine or butter, melted	1 cup sliced fresh strawberries
1 quart vanilla ice cream, softened	¹/₂ cup halved seedless red grapes
1¹/₂ pints orange sherbet, softened	3 tablespoons orange liqueur

To prepare crust, mix together cookie crumbs and margarine or butter. Press into a 10-inch pie plate. Bake in preheated 350° F oven for 5 minutes. Cool.

To prepare filling, spoon ice cream alternately with sherbet in crust and swirl to blend. Place in freezer and freeze until firm.

About 1 hour before serving, cut papaya into halves, remove seeds, and scoop out balls. Place prepared fresh fruits in a bowl. Add orange liqueur and chill for 1 hour. To serve, place fresh fruit topping on pie slices and serve immediately.

MAKES 6 TO 8 SERVINGS

CANNOLI CLOUD DESSERT

*Ricotta cheese is sweetened and studded with
chocolate chip bits, then served as a topping for a fresh
fruit dessert.*

15 ounces ricotta cheese
1/2 cup sifted confectioners
   sugar
2 tablespoons orange
   liqueur
1 teaspoon vanilla extract

1/4 cup mini semisweet
   chocolate chips
1 papaya
1 1/2 cups honeydew melon
   balls
1 cup fresh blueberries

In a small bowl, combine ricotta cheese, confectioners sugar,
liqueur, and vanilla, stirring to blend. Add chocolate chips to the
cheese mixture. Peel, seed, and dice the papaya. In a large bowl,
combine papaya, honeydew, and blueberries. Place fruit in 4
sherbet dishes. Top with cheese mixture.

MAKES 4 SERVINGS

FROZEN PAPAYA DAIQUIRI

1 papaya
4 ounces light rum
1/4 cup fresh lime juice

2 tablespoons sugar
8–10 ice cubes
   Lime slices for garnish

Cut papaya into halves, remove the seeds, and coarsely chop.
Combine all the ingredients except lime slices in a blender. Blend
until smooth. Pour into cocktail glasses. Garnish with lime slices.

MAKES 4 SERVINGS

PASSION FRUIT

This tropical fruit belongs to the Passiflora species. Members of this species have striking, uniquely designed flowers, which some believe symbolize the Passion of Christ. When Spanish missionaries to the Passiflora's native South America first saw these distinctive flowers, the stigmas, stamens, crown leaves, and sepals of the bloom symbolized to them elements of Christ's Passion—the wounds, crucifixion nails, crown of thorns, and the Apostles. The missionaries interpreted the presence of the Passiflora so symbolically as divine inspiration that they began converting the natives to Christianity!

Passion fruit is round to oval and can be purple, red, or gold. Inside its thin, but hard, cardboardlike shell is a translucent mass of juicy, golden capsules, containing tiny, crisp, edible dark seeds.

AVAILABILITY: Passion fruit is grown in California, Florida, Australia, New Zealand, and other regions around the world. As a result, supplies are available year round from various producers.

SELECTION AND STORAGE: Select large, heavy fruits. Passion fruit is ready to eat when the shell dimples, but still remains quite firm. Florida varieties tend to wrinkle less and are generally larger with a softer skin than other varieties. Keep at room temperature for a few days until dimpled. Once ripe, the fruit can be refrigerated for about one week. Passion fruit can also be placed in plastic bags and frozen for longer storage. The pulp can be scooped from the fruit, placed in covered freezer containers, and frozen for several months.

PREPARATION: Cut ripe fruit crosswise in half and scoop out the contents with a spoon. Five to six fruits yield about ½ cup pulp.

SERVING SUGGESTIONS:

- Lightly sweeten the fruit and use as a topping for fresh fruit, vanilla or fruit ice creams, or yogurt, or blend passion fruit pulp with sweetened whipped cream for a richer flavor.
- Flavor fruit, poultry, or gelatin salads with passion fruit.
- Add a tropical splash of flavor to drinks—the passion fruit's special flavoring qualities are perfect for punches and drinks, with or without alcohol.

NUTRITION INFORMATION: One fruit has a fair amount of vitamin C, is low in sodium, and contains about 18 calories.

PASSION FRUIT NECTAR

*The fragrant essence of passion fruit is locked up in the
juicy pulp surrounding the seeds. To capture more of the
juice from these tropical lovelies, use this easy technique.
The nectar adds an alluring accent to fresh fruit beverages,
frosty drinks, and cocktails, or as the base for the
Velvet Passion topping in the next recipe.*

5–6 passion fruit	*¹/₄ cup boiling water*

Cut off the top of each fruit and scoop contents into a sieve set over
a bowl. In a cup or bowl, combine the contents from the sieve with
the boiling water; allow to set about 5 minutes. Strain mixture
through the sieve, adding to the juice in the bowl. Use immediately, or cover and refrigerate or freeze.

MAKES ¹/₂ CUP

VELVET PASSION

*Try this easy, creamy topping spooned over fresh fruit,
poached pears, or angel or pound cake.*

¹/₃ cup Passion Fruit Nectar (see preceding recipe)	³/₄ cup milk
¹/₄ cup sugar	1 egg yolk
2 tablespoons cornstarch	¹/₄ cup light cream
Pinch of salt	¹/₂ teaspoon vanilla extract

Prepare Passion Fruit Nectar as directed in preceeding recipe;
measure ¹/₃ cup and reserve.

In a small saucepan, combine sugar, cornstarch, and salt. Stir in about 2 tablespoons of milk and mix until smooth. Gradually stir in remaining milk and cook over medium heat, stirring constantly until mixture thickens. Continue cooking about 1 minute more. Remove from heat.

Beat the yolk and stir it into the reserved Passion Fruit Nectar. Stir 3–4 tablespoons of the hot mixture into the passion fruit mixture; stirring until smooth. Gradually add the passion fruit mixture to the saucepan and cook over low heat until mixture begins to boil. Remove from heat and scrape into a bowl. Set the bowl into a larger bowl filled halfway with ice. Whisk in cream and vanilla. Cover and chill.

MAKES ABOUT 1 1/3 CUPS

PASSION FRUIT SAUCE

Try this easy sauce drizzled over boneless chicken breasts, turkey cutlets, pork medallions, or seafood.

2 large passion fruit	2 teaspoons sugar
1 1/2 tablespoons rum	1/4 teaspoon cornstarch
1 tablespoon fresh lemon juice	1 tablespoon margarine or butter

Cut passion fruit into halves; scoop out seeds and pulp and place in a blender. Whirl a few seconds then strain through a sieve.* Combine purée with rum, lemon juice, sugar, and cornstarch; stir to mix well.

---

* If you like an extra crunchy texture, there's no need to strain the seeds. Without straining, the sauce is studded with ground peppercorn-like bits. You might try this sauce first strained, adding a few of the ground seeds to sample.

In a small saucepan, melt the margarine or butter. Pour in the passion fruit mixture and cook over medium heat, stirring until the sauce thickens slightly. Serve immediately over meat, poultry, or seafood.

MAKES ABOUT ¼ CUP SAUCE, ENOUGH FOR TOPPING TWO ENTRÉES

PASSION FRUIT DRESSING

This tangy vinaigrette with its tropical accent is particularly good drizzled over watercress, mâche, or spinach in combination with slices of tropical fruits, such as carambola, mango, papaya, and avocado. The ground passion fruit seeds add crunchy texture.

2 large passion fruit
¼ cup fresh lime juice
   Grated peel from one
   large lime

4 teaspoons sugar
⅓ cup corn oil
   Salt

Halve passion fruits and scoop out seeds and pulp; place in a blender. Whirl mixture until the seeds resemble coarsely ground pepper. Add lime juice, peel, sugar, and oil; whirl until well-blended. Season with salt to taste.

MAKES 1 CUP

NOTE: The seeds can be strained if you find the added crunchiness objectionable.

TROPICAL SMOOTHIE

*1 large passion fruit or 2
  tablespoons Passion Fruit
  Nectar (see recipe on page
  195)*
1 ripe banana

*¹/₂ cup milk
1 tablespoon sugar
4–5 ice cubes (¹/₂ cup
  cracked ice)*

Halve passion fruit and scoop out pulp and liquid; place in blender. Purée fruit, strain, and discard seeds; return purée to blender. Combine strained passion fruit or Passion Fruit Nectar in a blender with the banana, milk, sugar, and ice. Blend until smooth.

MAKES 2 CUPS

$\mathcal{P}$ERSIMMON

The brilliant orange, smooth-skinned persimmon adds a sunburst of color to the produce department. Of Far East origin, seeds of the Oriental persimmon tree were brought to the U.S. from Japan in the 1800s, probably during one of Admiral Perry's expeditions.

The native American persimmon (Diospyros virgin-iana) was one of the first fruits praised by early explorers, but today is of no commercial importance. The two major persimmon varieties found in American supermarkets are of Oriental origin—the Hachiya and the Fuyu, also imported into the U.S. from Israel as the Sharon fruit.

The Hachiya (Hy-chee-a) is heart-shaped and very sweet when ripe; unripe it is bitterly astringent due to the presence of tannin. Ripening at room temperature will bring the Hachiya to its most sweet and delicate flavor.

The round, tomato-shaped Fuyu has a flattened bottom. Fuyus are crisp-textured, similar to an apple, and retain their crispness when cooked.

AVAILABILITY: October to December; the Fuyulike Sharon fruit is on the market chiefly mid-December through February.

SELECTION AND STORAGE: The Hachiya and Fuyu have different selection and handling requirements.

Hachiya: A beautiful glowing, bright orange color is not a sign of ripeness. Hachiyas are often marketed very firm, which requires additional ripening at home. Store at room temperature (or in a paper bag for quicker ripening) until it gives easily to gentle palm pressure and begins to look translucent. Full ripening may require 3–6 days. Once ripe, Hachiyas can be refrigerated and should be used promptly.

Fuyu: Look for a bright, deep orange color. In the market they are ripe and ready to eat. If kept at room temperature, Fuyus will soften, but never to the same extent as Hachiyas. They can be stored in the refrigerator up to 1 month.

PREPARATION: Persimmons don't need to be peeled, but if you prefer, an easy method is to place them in boiling water for 30–60 seconds, then plunge into cold water. The skins will easily slip off.

To purée, cut ripe fruit in half and scoop out pulp; discard stems, seeds, and skin. Place pulp in food processor or blender and process until smooth. One large Hachiya yields about $3/4-1$ cup purée.

To freeze, place ripe fruit in a single layer on a dish. When completely frozen, enclose in plastic bags; they should keep for several months. The pulp from ripe Hachiya varieties can be scooped out and combined with 1 teaspoon lemon or lime juice per cup of purée. Pack in airtight containers and freeze.

SERVING SUGGESTIONS:

- Add slices of either variety to fruit salads; Fuyus have a star-shaped center when sliced crosswise.
- Try a natural "sherbet." Wrap ripe fruit and freeze. Before serving, partially thaw a few hours in the refrigerator, but avoid thawing completely. Spoon frozen pulp from the skin or try it drizzled with an orange or nut-flavored liqueur.
- Purée ripe fruit for puddings, breads, pies, and more.
- Serve as a breakfast fruit or snack. Eat Fuyus out of hand or scoop chilled Hachiya pulp from the skin using a spoon and accent with fresh lemon or lime juice.
- Slice in a petallike fashion, drizzle with a little nut or orange liqueur, and garnish with a zest of lemon for a quick dessert.
- For a main dish accompaniment, halve fruit, dot with margarine or butter, and sprinkle with cinnamon and brown sugar. Broil halves just until the sugar bubbles.
- Crisp Fuyus can be used in many of the same recipes associated with apples.

NUTRITION INFORMATION: Both the Fuyu and Hachiya are good sources of vitamins A and C. A medium fruit has 118 calories.

PERSIMMON CHEESE PIE

*A no-roll piecrust spiced with cinnamon and layered with
sweetened cream cheese and a persimmon custard.*

Cinnamon Crust (recipe
   follows)
8 ounces cream cheese,
   softened
$^1/_2$ cup granulated sugar,
   divided
3 eggs, divided
$^1/_2$ teaspoon vanilla extract

1 pound ripe persimmons
$^1/_3$ cup firmly packed brown
   sugar
$^2/_3$ cup light cream or
   evaporated milk
1 teaspoon ground
   cinnamon

Prepare Cinnamon Crust. Set aside to cool.

In a medium bowl, combine the cream cheese and $^1/_4$ cup sugar,
beating well. Add 1 egg and the vanilla and beat until smooth.
Spoon into the baked Cinnamon Crust. Chill for 1 hour.

When cheese filling has chilled, prepare persimmon filling. Cut
persimmons into halves, scoop out flesh, and purée in a blender or
food processor. Measure enough to equal 1 cup. Add remaining 2
eggs and remaining $^1/_4$ cup granulated sugar, the brown sugar,
light cream or evaporated milk, and cinnamon; blend well. Pour
mixture over cheese filling. Bake at 350° F for 1 hour or until
done. Chill thoroughly before serving.

MAKES 6 TO 8 SERVINGS

CINNAMON CRUST

1 1/2 cups sifted flour
2 tablespoons sugar
3/4 teaspoon ground
    cinnamon

6 tablespoons margarine or
    butter, melted
1 egg
1 tablespoon cold water

In a medium bowl, mix the flour, sugar, and cinnamon together. Melt the margarine or butter and cut into the flour mixture. Beat the egg; add the egg and water to the bowl and mix well. Shape the mixture into a ball and place in a 10-inch pie plate; press dough on the bottom and sides of the pie plate. Prick the dough with a fork along the sides and the bottom. Bake in preheated 400° F oven for 10 minutes. Remove from oven and cool before filling.

PERSIMMON PECAN CREAM ROLL

A persimmon cake layer is topped with a pecan cheese filling and rolled into a superb moist dessert.

1/4 cup milk
2 teaspoons white vinegar
2 eggs
1 cup sugar
3/4 pound ripe persimmons
3/4 cup all-purpose flour
1 teaspoon baking powder
2 teaspoons ground
    cinnamon
1 teaspoon ground ginger

1/2 teaspoon salt
1 teaspoon fresh lemon
    juice
1 teaspoon vanilla extract
    Confectioners sugar as
    needed
    Pecan-Cheese Filling
    (recipe follows)
    Whipped cream

In a mixing bowl, combine the milk and vinegar. Beat in the eggs. Gradually add the sugar, beating well after each addition. Cut persimmons into halves, scoop out pulp, and purée in a blender or food processor. Measure $3/4$ cup purée. Add the purée to the egg mixture and beat well. Mix together flour, baking powder, cinnamon, ginger, and salt. Stir into the persimmon mixture. Add lemon juice and vanilla; beat well.

Line a lightly oiled 10-inch by 15-inch baking sheet with wax paper; lightly butter the paper. Spread persimmon mixture over the wax paper. Bake at 375° F for 15 minutes. Remove from oven and turn onto a linen towel well-coated with confectioners sugar. Carefully remove wax paper from cake and roll cake in the towel to cool. Cool for about 30 minutes. Unroll cake and spread pecan-cheese filling on top of it. Immediately reroll without the towel. Place in fresh wax paper and chill. To serve, cut into slices and top with whipped cream.

MAKES 6 SERVINGS

PECAN-CHEESE FILLING

6 ounces cream cheese, softened

$3/4$ cup sifted confectioners sugar

1 teaspoon fresh lemon juice

$1/2$ cup chopped pecans

In a small bowl, beat cheese until fluffy. Add confectioners sugar and lemon juice, beating well. Stir in pecans. Spread mixture on the partially cooled cake layer.

PERSIMMON PUDDING WITH BRANDY SAUCE

1 pound ripe persimmons
2/3 cup firmly packed brown
   sugar
4 tablespoons margarine or
   butter, melted
1/2 cup milk
1 egg
1 cup all-purpose flour

2 teaspoons baking powder
1/4 teaspoon salt
1/2 teaspoon ground
   cinnamon
1/4 teaspoon ground cloves
   Brandy Sauce (recipe
   follows)

Cut persimmons into halves and scoop out the pulp. Purée in a blender or food processor. Measure 1 cup purée. Combine purée, brown sugar, margarine or butter, milk, and egg. Beat until well-blended. In a small mixing bowl combine flour, baking powder, salt, and spices; add to persimmon batter and beat until smooth. Pour into a buttered 1 1/2-quart baking dish. Bake covered in a preheated 375° F oven for 50–55 minutes, or until set. Serve warm with Brandy Sauce.

MAKES 4 TO 6 SERVINGS

BRANDY SAUCE

1/2 cup butter
1 1/2 cups sifted confectioners
   sugar

1/4 cup brandy

In a saucepan, melt the butter. Add confectioners sugar and mix well. Stir in brandy and blend until smooth. Heat mixture through. Drizzle over pudding while warm.

PERSIMMON RAISIN-NUT BREAD

²/₃ cup sugar
¹/₂ cup margarine
2 eggs
1 teaspoon grated lemon
   peel
³/₄ teaspoon ground
   cinnamon
¹/₄ teaspoon ground cloves

1 pound ripe persimmons
1³/₄ cups all-purpose flour
2¹/₄ teaspoons baking
   powder
¹/₂ teaspoon salt
1¹/₂ cups raisins
¹/₂ cup chopped walnuts

In a large mixing bowl, cream together sugar and margarine. Beat eggs and stir into creamed mixture. Add lemon peel and spices. Cut persimmons into halves and scoop out flesh, removing any seeds. Purée in a blender or food processor until smooth. Measure 1 cup purée. Stir purée into creamed mixture.

In a small bowl, sift together flour, baking powder, and salt. Stir into persimmon mixture. Fold in raisins and nuts. Turn into a 9-inch by 5-inch loaf pan which has been coated with a nonstick cooking spray. Bake at 350° F for 1 hour, or until done. Cool slightly before turning out of pan.

MAKES 1 LOAF

GLAZED FUYU SLICES

Crisp-textured Fuyus make a perfect accompaniment to poultry or meat, sautéed and spiced with cinnamon and cloves.

4 small Fuyu persimmons
3 tablespoons margarine or
  butter
2 tablespoons sugar
¹/₄ teaspoon ground
  cinnamon

Pinch of ground cloves
2 teaspoons fresh lemon juice
2 tablespoons raisins

Remove leaves from stem end; peel fruit. Cut fruit crosswise into ¹/₄-inch slices (if using large fruit, cut slices into halves); discard any seeds.

In a medium skillet, melt margarine or butter over medium heat. Stir in sugar, spices, and lemon juice, mixing well. Add Fuyu slices and raisins. Cook over low heat, stirring occasionally, until fruit is lightly glazed and hot. Serve warm.

MAKES 4 TO 6 SERVINGS

SZECHWAN CHICKEN SALAD WITH FUYUS AND HONEY-SESAME CRESCENTS

Substitute 3 Fuyu persimmons for the Asian pears in the recipe on page 30. Thinly slice Fuyus crosswise to reveal the star-shaped design and arrange on salad.

FUYUS WITH CREAMY ALMOND TOPPING

Substitute 3 Fuyu persimmons for the Asian pears in recipe on page 32, cutting them crosswise into thin slices. Arrange slices on 4 individual dessert plates in a circular pattern and drizzle with the liqueur. Place a dollop of the topping in the center and garnish with the toasted almonds.

$\mathcal{P}$EPINO

This subtropical fruit, also known as the pepino melon or melon pear, is a newcomer to produce departments. When ripe, the pepino's satiny-smooth skin is streaked with purple and either a golden yellow or pinkish-apricot. The tear-shaped pepino can be 2–4 inches long.

The flesh color ranges from a pale yellowish-green to a yellowish-orange. It has a juicy and melonlike texture, but it is not as sweet as cantaloupe or honeydew.

Originally from South America, this subtle-flavored fruit has traveled the world and has become popular in the Orient. The pepino is one of the most beloved fruits in Japan.

AVAILABILITY: With crops from California, Chile, and New Zealand, pepinos are available nearly year round.

SELECTION AND STORAGE: Check for a sweet, fragrant aroma. Pepinos generally require additional ripening to bring them to their fullest flavor. When still firm and streaked with green, pepinos must be kept at room temperature until the green striations turn golden and the fruit yields to gentle pressure, but is not soft. Once ripe, the fruit can be refrigerated, but plan to use it within a few days.

PREPARATION: Pepinos are best chilled. Cut into halves, discard the seeds, then scoop out or slice the fruit and add sweetening if desired. Although its thin skin is edible, it is better to peel the fruit.

SERVING SUGGESTIONS: Use as other melons, served with a squeeze of fresh lemon or lime juice, combined into salads and fruit compotes, or used as a natural vessel for holding salads. Accent its flavor with ginger or mint.

NUTRITION INFORMATION: Pepinos are an excellent source of vitamin C, provide vitamin A and other nutrients, are low in sodium, and contain just 33 calories per $3^1/2$ ounces.

MINI MELON BERRY BOATS

Chilled lime syrup adds zesty flavor to pint-size pepinos and berries.

2 tablespoons sugar	4 pepino melons, each about
Grated lime peel from	6–8 ounces
½ large lime	2 cups mixed fresh berries
1½ tablespoons fresh lime	(raspberries, blueberries,
juice	sliced strawberries)
2 tablespoons water	Fresh mint or lemon balm

In a small saucepan, combine sugar, lime peel, juice, and water. Bring mixture to a boil; boil 2 minutes. Remove from heat; chill at least 30 minutes.

Cut pepinos into halves and scoop out seeds; place melon halves on a serving plate or 4 individual salad plates. Divide berries among melon halves. Drizzle each half with some of the chilled lime syrup. Garnish with mint or lemon balm.

MAKES 4 SERVINGS

SPICED HAZELNUT PEPINOS

¼ cup shelled hazelnuts	4 pepinos, each about 6–8
2 tablespoons sugar	ounces
½ teaspoon ground	Juice of one lime
cinnamon	Red grape clusters

Place hazelnuts in a pie plate. Toast nuts in preheated 400° F oven about 7–9 minutes or until lightly browned, stirring a few times while toasting. Remove from oven and rub nuts in a towel to remove as much of their brown skins. When cool, grind nuts in a blender or food processor. In a small bowl, combine ground nuts, sugar, and cinnamon.

Cut pepinos into halves. Scoop out seeds. Squeeze a little lime juice over each half. Sprinkle about 2 teaspoons of the hazelnut mixture over each half. Place 2 halves on 4 individual salad plates and garnish with grape clusters.

MAKES 4 SERVINGS

$\mathcal{P}$LANTAIN

The plantain, also known as the cooking banana or plátano, resembles a large banana with tapering ends. At each stage of maturity the plantain provides entirely different flavor, texture, and preparation ideas. Unlike bananas, plantains must be cooked before eating.

The plantain is "the potato of the tropics," and is commonly prepared in the Caribbean, Central and South America, Africa, and the tropical Far East. They are imported to the U.S. from Central America, the Caribbean, and Mexico.

Plantains can be eaten at each stage of maturity—from green-skinned and unripe to fully black-skinned and ripe.

The fruit itself ranges in color from creamy white, yellow-ish, or tinged with pink.

Green, or unripe, plantains are quite starchy, similar in flavor to the potato and are used as vegetables. At this stage, they are excellent sliced wafer-thin, deep-fried, and served as a crisp chip.

As plantains ripen, they become sweeter and softer. When yellow-skinned, plantains are still starchy and are not yet sweet as their banana counterparts. As they ripen from yellow-brown to black, they acquire more sweetness and a banana aroma.

Ripe plantains are delicious simply sautéed in butter or margarine and served with a wedge of fresh lemon or lime juice. They can also be baked, broiled, or grilled and served as a meat, poultry, or seafood accompaniment. Black-ripe plantains can be cooked to dessert perfection, sautéed, and blanketed in a buttery brown sugar sauce.

AVAILABILITY: Year round.

SELECTION AND STORAGE: Plantains are sold individually and are offered for sale at varying stages of ripeness. Skin color ranges from green when unripe to dark brown or black when ripe.

Plantains are slow to ripen. Green plantains take 2–3 weeks to ripen fully and should be stored at room temperature. Refrigeration stops the ripening process altogether. Ripe plantains can be refrigerated, but will continue to keep without refrigeration a week or more.

PREPARATION: Ripe plantains can be peeled, like bananas. However, the peel of green or yellow plantains clings to the fruit, making it difficult to remove. To peel a green plantain, slice off the tips and cut the plantain crosswise into halves. Make four lengthwise slits in each half from one end to the other. Pull the skin away, one strip at a time, pulling crosswise rather than lengthwise.

SERVING SUGGESTIONS:

- Sauté slices of yellow or yellowish-brown–skinned plantain in oil until golden brown and serve as a vegetable accompaniment.
- Simmer chunks of partially ripe plantains in soups and stews.
- Thinly slice green-skinned plantains and fry until crisp for plantain chips.
- Cook and mash ripe plantains, then combine with diced apple or mashed sweetpotato.

NUTRITION INFORMATION: Plantains provide potassium, vitamin B6, and vitamin C. A 3½-ounce serving is low in sodium and provides about 116 calories.

CRISPY GOLDEN PLANTAINS

2 black-ripe plantains   1½ cups crushed cornflakes
2 eggs, beaten

Peel the plantains and slice crosswise into halves, then lengthwise into quarters. Dip plantain slices into the beaten egg, then roll them in cornflakes and thoroughly coat with the crumbs. Place in a buttered or lightly oiled shallow baking dish. Cover and bake in preheated 425° F oven for 15–20 minutes, or until tender.

MAKES 4 TO 6 SERVINGS

PLANTAIN CHIPS

Green plantains are sliced thin and fried crisp like
potato chips.

2 green plantains   Salt
1/2 cup vegetable oil

Peel the plantains and cut crosswise into 1/8-inch-thick slices. In a
large skillet, heat oil over medium-high heat. Add half the plantain
slices and fry for about 5 minutes on each side, or until crisp and
golden brown. Drain on paper towels. Add remaining slices and
cook as above. Sprinkle with salt to taste. Cool thoroughly before
storage. Store in an airtight container.

MAKES 4 TO 6 SERVINGS

DESSERT PLANTAIN DELIGHT

Very ripe plantains are necessary for this sweet dessert
creation.

2 black-ripe plantains   3/4 teaspoon ground
4 tablespoons margarine or   cinnamon
    butter   2 tablespoons light rum
6 ounces cream cheese,   3/4 cup heavy cream
    softened   Vanilla ice cream or
3 tablespoons brown sugar   frozen yogurt (optional)

Peel the plantains, cut crosswise into halves, and slice sections
lengthwise into thirds. Melt margarine or butter in a large skillet.

Sauté plantain slices until lightly browned on both sides. Arrange slices in an 8-inch-square baking dish. Set aside.

In a medium bowl, beat cream cheese until fluffy. Add brown sugar, cinnamon, and rum; beat well. Spread cheese mixture over plantains. Pour heavy cream over cheese topping. Bake in preheated 375° F oven for 20 minutes, or until lightly browned. Serve warm with a dollop of whipped cream or ice cream, if desired.

MAKES 4 SERVINGS

PLANTAINS CARIBE

6 tablespoons margarine or
  butter
1/3 cup firmly packed dark
  brown sugar
1/4 cup dry red wine

1 tablespoon water
1 teaspoon ground cinnamon
2 black-ripe plantains
4 scoops of vanilla ice cream
  or frozen yogurt

Melt the margarine or butter in a medium skillet. Add the brown sugar, wine, water, and cinnamon; stir to blend. Peel the plantains and slice crosswise into halves, then lengthwise into quarters. Add sliced plantains to the skillet. Simmer uncovered, stirring frequently, for 10–15 minutes, or until plantains are tender. Serve warm over vanilla ice cream or frozen yogurt.

MAKES 4 SERVINGS

PLANTAIN-SESAME CIRCLES WITH HONEY-LIME SAUCE

Ripe plantain slices are blanketed with sesame seeds and sautéed until golden brown. Serve these hot with a honey lime sauce for dipping.

Honey-Lime Sauce
(recipe follows)
1/2 *cup flour*
1/4 *cup sesame seeds*
1/4 *teaspoon salt*

2 *medium-size, black-ripe plantains*
1/3 *cup milk*
4 *tablespoons peanut oil*

Prepare Honey-Lime Sauce and set aside.

In a large, shallow dish, combine flour, sesame seeds, and salt. Peel plantains and cut into 1/4-inch diagonal slices. Dip slices into milk, then roll in the sesame seed mixture, coating well.

In a large skillet, heat oil. Add plantain slices and cook over medium heat for about 2–3 minutes on one side or until golden; turn slices over and continue cooking on the other side until golden. If not all the slices can fit in the skillet at one time, add more oil to complete the cooking. Drain slices on paper towels. Serve hot with Honey-Lime Sauce.

MAKES 4 SERVINGS

HONEY-LIME SAUCE

1 *large lime*
1 *tablespoon cornstarch*
1/4 *cup honey*

1/3 *cup water*
Pinch of salt

Grate the peel from the lime. Squeeze juice and measure 2 tablespoons. In a small saucepan, combine lime peel, juice, and cornstarch; stir until smooth. Stir in honey, water, and salt. Bring mixture to a boil, stirring constantly until thickened. Allow to cool at least 10 minutes before serving.

MAKES ABOUT $2/3$ CUP

TROPICAL FRUIT AND SHRIMP STIR-FRY IN PINEAPPLE-RUM SAUCE

2 medium-size, black-ripe
  plantains
4 scallions
2 tablespoons sugar
2 teaspoons cornstarch
$1/4$ teaspoon ground allspice
$2/3$ cup unsweetened
  pineapple juice

3 tablespoons light or dark
  rum
4 tablespoons vegetable oil,
  divided
1 pound medium shrimp
1 cup diced fresh pineapple
1 cup diced fresh mango
  Shredded coconut
  Hot cooked rice

Peel plantains and cut into $1/4$-inch diagonal slices. Thinly slice scallions. Set ingredients aside.

In a cup or bowl, add the sugar, cornstarch, and allspice; stir in about half the pineapple juice and mix well to blend. Stir in remaining pineapple juice and rum; set aside.

In a large, nonstick skillet, heat 2 tablespoons oil. Add shrimp and sauté about 3 minutes over medium-high heat or until shrimp are opaque. Remove shrimp with a slotted spoon; set aside. Heat remaining 2 tablespoons oil. Add the plantains and sauté 3–4 minutes or until done. Stir in pineapple and mango; cook 1 minute.

Return shrimp to skillet; pour in the reserved pineapple-rum sauce, stirring just until the sauce thickens. Stir in the scallions. Transfer to a serving dish. Garnish with coconut. Serve immediately over hot cooked rice.

MAKES 4 SERVINGS

SAUTÉED PLANTAINS

A quick side dish packed with potassium!

2 medium-size yellow or
  black-ripe plantains

3 tablespoons vegetable oil
Salt

Peel plantains; cut crosswise into halves, then cut lengthwise into halves. Heat oil in a large skillet. Add plantains and cook over medium heat, about 4 minutes or until golden brown. Turn slices over and cook until golden brown on the other side. Drain on paper towels. Season with salt, if desired. Serve hot.

MAKES 4 SERVINGS

POMEGRANATE

This colorful, autumn fruit has an ancient history. It is entwined in mythology and legend and is even referred to in the Bible—King Solomon sang of "an orchard of pomegranates" and Moses described the Promised Land as a "land of wheat and barley, and vines and fig trees, and pomegranates."

The pomegranate's origin is Persia, but it has been cultivated for centuries in subtropical parts of Europe, Asia, and North Africa. The Spanish missionaries brought this refreshing fruit to California two centuries ago where it is now commercially cultivated.

The pomegranate has a hard, leathery, deep red to purplish rind and is about the same size as a large apple. In fact, its name comes from the Latin pomun granatum, meaning "apple of many seeds." When opened, the fruit bedazzles the beholder with its beautiful, shimmering, translucent kernels.

The prized asset of this naturally jeweled splendor is the juicy, translucent, tart-sweet pulp that surrounds each seed. The nutlike seed is also edible, adding a bit of crunch. These ruby kernels, which are encased within a spongy, white or cream-colored membrane that separates them into *clusters, are called arils. The membrane is bitter and should not be eaten.*

There is no perfect or tidy way to eat a pomegranate because of its juiciness. One method does help reduce the squirting for out-of-hand eating. Cut off the crown end from the top of the pomegranate. Then use a knife to score the skin in quarters, starting at the crown and continuing length-wise down the fruit. Be careful to score only the skin, avoid puncturing the fruit and releasing a gush of juice. Bend back the rind, peel away the white membrane from the clusters, and you're ready to savor the tart-sweet kernels.

AVAILABILITY: August through December, with peak supplies in October.

SELECTION AND STORAGE: Look for large pomegranates which tend to be juicier with better developed arils. Select fruit with a hard, unbroken rind. Pomegranates are ripe and ready to eat. They can be kept at room temperature for short periods, but for longer storage, refrigerate. Pomegranates store well in the refrigerator and can be kept for several months.

The kernels or arils can be frozen for extended use. Place kernels in a single layer and freeze until firm, then pack in airtight containers. They can be stored this way for up to 6 months. Spoon out the desired quantity and thaw or use them as a frozen snack.

PREPARATION: To remove the kernels, use the method outlined above for out-of-hand eating or try what I refer to as the "sink or swim" method which further eliminates squirting: Cut off the crown end of the pomegranate and score the rind lengthwise in several sections. Partially fill a sink with cool water and soak for about 5 minutes. Gently separate the clusters from the membrane, using your fingers. The membrane and rind floats to the top and the kernels to the bottom. Retrieve the kernels, drain, and pat dry.

Pomegranates are particularly noted for their distinctively tangy sweet juice. Using a blender or food processor to extract the juice is preferred to using a reamer or electric juicer, which can also extract some of the bitter pulp.

Place about 1½–2 cups of kernels in a food processor or blender and process until liquefied. Pour through a fine-meshed sieve and drain. The juice can be refrigerated for several days; frozen for several months. A medium pomegranate yields about ³/₄ cup seeds or ½ cup juice.

Serving Suggestions:

- The pomegranate's glistening seeds are a glorious accent scattered over all types of salads.
- Sprinkle seeds over puddings, yogurt, or ice cream.
- Prepare a pomegranate syrup (see recipe below) to add to beverages or pour over ice cream, yogurt, or other desserts for a splash of color and sweetness.
- Use as a garnish for poultry, fish, or meats.
- Freeze kernels and enjoy them frozen for a snack.

Nutrition Information: A pomegranate about 3½ inches in diameter provides potassium and vitamin C, is low in sodium, and contains about 100 calories. The seeds contribute to fiber intake.

POMEGRANATE SYRUP

Pomegranate juice combined with sugar syrup adds special flavoring and color to beverages.

8 *pomegranates, each about* 12 *ounces*	1 *cup sugar* ³/₄ *cup white corn syrup*

Remove kernels from pomegranates, discarding white membrane. Place kernels in a food processor and purée. Strain through a sieve and measure 2 cups juice.

In a large saucepan, combine the pomegranate juice, sugar, and corn syrup. Bring the mixture to a boil and cook for 8–10 minutes, or until syrup is slightly thickened. Remove from heat and skim off any foam. Pour into jars. For extended storage, pour into sterilized containers and seal.

MAKES 2¹/₂ CUPS

JEWELED FRUIT SALAD

²/₃ *cup mayonnaise*	2 *bananas*
¹/₄ *cup fresh orange juice*	2 *navel oranges*
2 *tablespoons sugar*	*Lettuce leaves*
Juice from 1 lemon	1 *pomegranate, about 12*
2 *red apples*	*ounces*

Combine the mayonnaise, orange juice, and sugar in a small bowl. Mix until well-blended; set aside. Squeeze lemon into a medium mixing bowl. Core and seed apples and cut into thin slices. Cut bananas into diagonal slices. Place sliced apples and bananas in bowl with the lemon juice; toss to coat. Peel the oranges and cut into rounds. Arrange the apples, bananas, and oranges on a bed of lettuce. Remove kernels from the pomegranate and sprinkle over fruits. Serve with reserved dressing.

MAKES 8 SERVINGS

CRIMSON DESSERT SAUCE

Spoon this colorful sauce over ice cream or slices of angel food, chiffon, or pound cake.

4 pomegranates, each about
12 ounces
3/4 cup sugar
1 tablespoon cornstarch
2 tablespoons fresh lemon
juice

2 tablespoons margarine or
butter
1 tablespoon brandy
(optional)

Remove kernels from pomegranates, discarding white membrane. Place kernels in a food processor and purée. Strain mixture; measure 1 cup juice.

In a medium saucepan, combine juice, sugar, and cornstarch. Bring mixture to a boil and cook until thickened to a syrup consistency, stirring frequently. Remove from heat. Stir in lemon juice and margarine or butter. Cool before adding brandy. Serve warm or chilled.

MAKES ABOUT 1 CUP

PORT O' POMEGRANATE PUNCH

¹/₂ cup port wine
¹/₄ cup fresh orange juice
¹/₄ cup Pomegranate Syrup
   (see recipe on page 221)

2 jiggers (3 ounces) brandy
Cracked ice
Orange wedges

In a cocktail shaker, combine wine, orange juice, syrup, and brandy. Pour over cracked ice. Garnish with orange wedges.

MAKES 2 COCKTAILS

THE BEACHCOMBER

1¹/₂ cups light or dark rum
³/₄ cup fresh Pomegranate
   Syrup (see recipe on
   page 221)

³/₄ cup fresh lime juice
2 cups club soda
Ice cubes
Fresh pineapple wedges

In a large pitcher, combine rum, Pomegranate Syrup, and lime juice. If possible, chill punch base before serving. To serve, pour club soda into punch base. Pour punch into tall glasses over ice. Garnish with pineapple.

MAKES 6 TO 8 SERVINGS

FESTIVE FRUIT PUNCH

3/4 cup sugar
3/4 cup water
4 pomegranates, each about
12 ounces
4 medium oranges
4 medium lemons

3/4 cup unsweetened
pineapple juice
2 cups club soda
Ice cubes
Fresh pineapple spears
for garnish

In a small saucepan, combine the sugar and water. Bring to a boil and cook for 8–10 minutes. Remove from heat and cool.

Remove kernels from pomegranates, discarding white membranes. Place kernels in a food processor; purée. Strain seeds and measure 1 cup juice.

Cut oranges and lemons into halves. Extract enough juice from oranges to equal 1 cup. Extract enough juice from lemons to equal 1/2 cup. In a blender or food processor, combine all fruit juices; blend well. Add sugar syrup to fruit juices. Chill mixture. Add club soda right before serving. Pour into tall glasses over ice cubes. Garnish glasses with pineapple spears.

MAKES 1 1/2 QUARTS

QUINCE

The quince is a fruit rich in romance and symbolism. In legend, it was dedicated to Aphrodite and Venus, the Greek and Roman goddesses of love, beauty, and fertility. The quince was used in ancient marriage ceremonies to symbolize love, happiness, and fertility. Some have even suggested that it was the "forbidden fruit" in the Garden of Eden.

The quince tree is native to Asia and cultivated for its ornamental qualities as well as for its extremely fragrant fruit. Botanically, the quince is a member of the rose family, a close relative of the apple and pear. In fact, quinces look like misshapen yellow or green apples and can be round, oval, or pear-shaped depending on the variety.

For centuries in kitchens around the world, the quince has been valued for its high content of pectin, a carbohydrate used in fruit jellies, pharmaceuticals, and cosmetics.

This fruit is one of the few that must be cooked because it is too tart, hard, and unpalatable raw. But by cooking and sweetening, the quince develops a rich flavor, attractive pink or mauve flesh, and appealing texture.

AVAILABILITY: Chiefly available during autumn, but can make appearances throughout winter.

SELECTION AND STORAGE: Choose large, firm, smooth fruit which are easier to peel than the smaller, more knobby fruits. As quinces ripen, they turn a pale yellow. Some may have a fuzz on the surface and they bruise easily, so handle them gently.

Quinces can be kept at room temperature for about a week. They will fill the room with their fragrant aroma. For longer storage, wrap in plastic and refrigerate. Quinces are well-adapted to long storage and can often be kept for several months.

PREPARATION: Quinces tend to be a little unyielding during preparation. The core, composed of parchmentlike compartments, is hard and takes patience to remove. Be sure to remove all of the core prior to cooking to eliminate a grainy texture.

SERVING SUGGESTIONS:

- Well-suited for jams, jellies, preserves, conserves, and fruit leather.
- Try quince poached, stewed, baked, or braised.
- Spice stewed slices with cinnamon and serve as a side dish.
- Purée cooked quince into a sauce, similar to applesauce in texture, but with more flavor.

NUTRITION INFORMATION: A 3½-ounce portion provides vitamin C, B-vitamins, fiber, potassium, and other nutrients, and contains about 57 calories.

CRANBERRY-QUINCE CRUMB DESSERT

3/4 cup sugar
3 tablespoons cornstarch
1/2 cup light corn syrup
1/4 cup water
3 cups fresh cranberries
2 quinces, each about 8
  ounces

1 1/2 teaspoons grated orange
  peel
2 tablespoons margarine
  or butter
  Cookie Crumb Topping
  (recipe follows)
  Vanilla ice cream

In a large saucepan, mix together sugar and cornstarch. Stir in the corn syrup and water. Cook over medium heat until mixture thickens slightly.

Rinse the cranberries; remove any stems. Peel, core, and dice the quinces. Add cranberries and quinces to the syrup mixture and cook for about 5 minutes, or until the cranberry skins break. Remove from heat; add orange peel and margarine or butter and stir until margarine or butter melts. Pour into an 8-inch-square baking dish which has been lightly coated with a nonstick cooking spray. Top with the Cookie Crumb Topping. Bake in preheated 375° F oven for 25–30 minutes. Serve warm with vanilla ice cream.

MAKES 6 SERVINGS

COOKIE CRUMB TOPPING

32 vanilla wafers
1/3 cup all-purpose flour
1/3 cup margarine or butter,
  softened

1 tablespoon sugar
1/2 teaspoon ground
  cinnamon

Crush enough vanilla wafers to make 1 cup. Mix together all ingredients until well blended. Sprinkle topping over cranberry-quince mixture.

QUINCE CRISP

4 quinces, each about 8
   ounces
3 tablespoons fresh lemon
   juice
2 tablespoons granulated
   sugar
1 teaspoon ground cinnamon

$^1/_2$ cup all-purpose flour
$^1/_2$ cup firmly packed brown
   sugar
4 tablespoons margarine or
   butter, softened
Vanilla ice cream or
   frozen yogurt

Peel and core the quinces and cut into thin slices. Place slices in an 8-inch-square baking dish. Squeeze the lemon juice over the slices. Mix the granulated sugar and cinnamon together and sprinkle over the quinces, tossing to coat the fruit.

In a medium mixing bowl, combine the flour, brown sugar, and margarine or butter. Using a pastry blender or 2 knives scissor-fashion, mix the ingredients until crumbly. Spread the crumb mixture over the quince slices, covering completely. Bake in pre-heated 375° F oven for 25–30 minutes. Serve warm with vanilla ice cream or frozen yogurt.

MAKES 4 TO 6 SERVINGS

QUINCE SAUCE

Quince sauce is reminiscent of applesauce but with its own distinctive flavor.

4 quinces, each about 8
    ounces
1 cup water
Juice of ¹/₂ fresh lemon

¹/₂ cup sugar
1 teaspoon ground
    cinnamon

Peel quinces and cut into slices, removing seeds and cores. Place quinces in a saucepan; add water and lemon juice. Simmer covered for about 15 minutes, or until tender. Purée fruit, including water, in a blender or food processor. Add sugar and cinnamon and blend well. Chill if desired.

MAKES 3 CUPS

RADICCHIO

Radicchio (rahd-EEk-ee-o), the Italian name for chicory, has long been a part of the European salad bowl and is achieving notoriety now wherever a good salad is appreci-

ated. Its vivid burgundy leaves and contrasting white ribs makes it a striking, decorative accent in salads.

But radicchio adds more than just color. As a member of the chicory family, radicchio has the characteristic bittersweet flavor so distinctive of its relatives Belgian endive, curly endive, and escarole.

AVAILABILITY: Year round.

SELECTION AND STORAGE: The heads are rather small in comparison to lettuce, which can be round or elongated depending on the variety. The round, *radicchio rosso*, or red Verona chicory, is shaped like a small cabbage. Red Treviso chicory is elongated, with spear-shaped leaves ranging in color from pink to deep red. *Radicchio de Castelfranco* and *radicchio di Chiogga* have variegated leaves of pink, green, or red and are similar to the Verona variety in size and shape.

When selecting radicchio, look for fresh-looking leaves without any browning along the edges. The white core at the base should be firm and unblemished.

Store heads loosely wrapped in the refrigerator. Use within one week for best flavor and crispness, although heads purchased in good condition will often keep longer.

PREPARATION: Remove the white central core. Separate the leaves and trim as necessary. Rinse leaves and blot dry with paper towels.

SERVING SUGGESTIONS:

- The sturdy heads make excellent baskets for dips and fruit, pasta, or poultry salads.

- Like other chicories, radicchio can be cooked—delicious, but it will lose its brillant color. Grill, bake, or sauté radicchio quarters or halves in olive oil or butter, flavored with garlic and herbs.
- Enliven all kinds of crisp salads with radicchio's scarlet leaves or sauté for a warm salad.

NUTRITION INFORMATION: Specific nutrient information is not available for radicchio, but the chicory family is a good source of vitamins A and C.

CASHEW CHICKEN AND CITRUS SALAD

A striking salad presentation accented with a colorful ring of radicchio leaves.

1 pound boneless, skinless chicken breasts
1/4 cup fresh orange juice
2 tablespoons vegetable oil
2 tablespoons minced fresh parsley or cilantro
1 tablespoon fresh lime juice
2 teaspoons sugar
2 teaspoons Dijon mustard
1/2 teaspoon grated orange peel
1/4 teaspoon salt
Radicchio leaves from one medium head
3/4 bunch of watercress
1 navel orange or tangelo
2 scallions
2–3 tablespoons cashews

Place chicken in a medium skillet, cover with water or chicken broth, and bring to a boil. Cover and cook over medium heat about 6–8 minutes or until chicken is done. Drain; cut chicken into 1/4-inch slices. Place chicken in a 1-quart casserole.

In a measuring cup or bowl, combine orange juice, oil, parsley or cilantro, lime juice, sugar, mustard, orange peel, and salt. Stir to blend; pour over chicken. Cover and chill for at least 30 minutes.

At serving time, wash radicchio and separate the leaves. Arrange leaves in a circle all around the edge of two dinner plates. Rinse watercress and discard the thick stems; place in center of the plate. Peel the orange or tangelo; separate into sections and cut sections crosswise into halves. Thinly slice scallions. Toss orange or tangelo sections and scallions with the chicken. Mound chicken mixture over the watercress, drizzling dressing over greens. Garnish salad with cashews.

MAKES 2 MAIN-DISH SERVINGS

CAESAR SALAD WITH GRILLED BEEF TENDERLOIN AND ROASTED RED PEPPERS

1/4 cup olive or corn oil
1 tablespoon fresh lemon juice
2 teaspoons Worcestershire sauce
1 teaspoon Dijon mustard
1 garlic clove, minced
2 anchovies, finely cut (optional)
Salt
8 ounces beef tenderloin
Coarsely ground black pepper
3 cups torn romaine lettuce
1 cup torn radicchio leaves
1/2 cup grated Parmesan cheese
1/2 cup garlic croutons Marinated Roasted Red Peppers (recipe follows)

In a screw-top jar, combine oil, lemon juice, Worcestershire sauce, mustard, garlic, anchovies, and salt. Shake well to blend; set aside. (This mixture can be prepared several hours in advance.)

Trim the beef of fat and season with black pepper. Cook beef on grill or in broiler until medium-rare. Remove from grill or broiler. Allow to stand while assembling salad.

Rinse lettuce and radicchio; pat dry and place in a large salad bowl. Add cheese. Pour dressing over salad; toss well. Divide salad on 2 dinner plates; sprinkle with croutons. Thinly slice beef and arrange over lettuce. Season salad with pepper to taste and garnish with Marinated Roasted Red Peppers.

MAKES 2 SERVINGS

MARINATED ROASTED RED PEPPERS

1 medium red bell pepper
2 tablespoons olive oil
1 tablespoon red or white vinegar

1 garlic clove, minced
1/2 teaspoon dried tarragon
1/8 teaspoon salt

Place the pepper on a baking sheet and roast under a broiler, cooking just until the skin is blistered and lightly browned on all sides. Remove from oven. Cover pepper with a damp paper towel. When cool enough to handle, peel off skin. Cut off the stem end and slice the pepper lengthwise; remove seeds and membrane. Thinly slice pepper and place in a small bowl. Combine olive oil, vinegar, garlic, tarragon, and salt; pour over pepper. Cover and refrigerate until serving time.

MAKES 2 SERVINGS

$\mathcal{R}$APINI

Also known as Broccoli Rabe, Broccoli Raab, Choy Sum, Chinese Flowering Cabbage, this zesty green has been a favorite of Italian and Chinese cooks. Like other traditional ethnic items, this nonheading broccoli is branching out, being greeted with some caution, but winning acclaim along the way.

Rapini's taste is bitter, yet lively, and may require some adjustment for the more subdued tastebuds. It is particularly welcomed in combination with mild-flavored foods, such as pastas and potatoes, but it also adds dynamic contrast to other equally assertive foods.

AVAILABILITY: Year round, with peak supplies during the fall and winter.

SELECTION AND STORAGE: Choose bunches with relatively small stems. The heads range in size from a quarter to a silver dollar. Keep wrapped in plastic, refrigerated, and use within a few days.

PREPARATION: Rapini must be cooked before eating. The stems, leaves, and heads are all edible. Just slice off the very end of the stems to freshen, then briefly steam, stir-fry, braise, micro-wave, or boil. Keep cooking time short, between 2–6 minutes depending on the selected cooking technique. For a less assertive taste, blanch the greens about one minute in boiling salted water, drain, and prepare by preferred cooking method.

SERVING SUGGESTIONS:

- Combine cooked rapini with sliced carrots, flavored with lemon juice and a little olive oil.
- Toss it into pasta combinations, served warm or chilled.
- Add to stir-fry recipes, lightly glazed with oyster sauce.
- Sauté in olive oil with minced garlic and chili peppers.

NUTRITION INFORMATION: An excellent source of vitamins A and C, a $1/2$-cup serving is free of sodium and has less than 30 calories.

ORIENTAL SCALLOPS AND RAPINI

1 pound rapini
1 (1-inch) piece fresh ginger
1 (9-ounce) package fresh
   fettucine
3 tablespoons rice wine
   vinegar
2 tablespoons reduced-
   sodium soy sauce

1 tablespoon honey
$1/2$ teaspoon sesame oil
2 tablespoons margarine or
   butter
1 garlic clove, minced
1 pound sea scallops
$1/4$ cup chopped red bell
   pepper

Rinse rapini and pat dry. Trim and discard any yellow or coarse leaves and any tough stem ends; cut into 1-inch pieces. Peel ginger and cut into thin strips.

Boil pasta in boiling water for 2–3 minutes or until *al dente*. Drain well and transfer to a serving platter; keep warm.

Drop rapini into a large kettle of salted boiling water. Return to a boil over high heat; boil 1 minute or until crisp-tender. Drain well; set aside and keep warm.

In a measuring cup or bowl, combine vinegar, soy sauce, honey, and sesame oil; set aside.

In a large skillet, heat 1 tablespoon margarine or butter. Add pepper and sauté until crisp-tender. Set aside and keep warm. Heat remaining margarine or butter in skillet. Add garlic and ginger and sauté about 30 seconds. Add scallops and cook until opaque. Add rapini and cook until thoroughly heated. Add vinegar mixture; toss well. Spoon scallops and sauce over center of fettucine. Sprinkle with chopped pepper and serve immediately.

MAKES 4 SERVINGS

GARLIC RAPINI

Pungent, assertive flavor of rapini is supported by garlic and hot pepper.

1 pound rapini	Salt
3 cloves garlic	Coarsely ground black
1–2 jalapeño peppers	pepper
3 tablespoons olive oil	

Rinse rapini and pat dry. Trim and discard any yellow coarse leaves and the tough stem ends. Peel and thinly slice the garlic. Remove membrane and seeds from pepper; finely chop pepper.

Add rapini to a large pot of boiling water. Return to a boil over high heat. Boil 1–2 minutes or until crisp-tender. Drain well.

In a large skillet; heat the oil. Add the garlic and jalapeño; sauté 30 seconds. Add the rapini. Cook until thoroughly heated, tossing gently. Season to taste with salt and pepper.

MAKES 4 SERVINGS

RHUBARB

Rhubarb's historical roots date back to as early as 2700 B.C., when its root was revered as a medicinal herb. This species was carried from the Far East into Russia where it received its name. Rhubarb is derived from the Latin Rha barbarum, which means "Rha of the barbarians." Rha was the name of the river, now called the Volga, along whose banks the plant was cultivated by the barbarians.

During the Middle Ages, the Asian variety of rhubarb was still valued for medicinal attributes and used in European apothecaries. Edible rhubarb is a native of Siberia and traditionally has been a harbinger of spring. Russian fur traders introduced rhubarb to America by the eighteenth century. Europeans did not eat the Siberian variety of rhubarb until late in the eighteenth century. Benjamin Franklin took a fancy to the ruby stalks while visiting Scotland and sent seeds back to the American colonies.

Botanically, rhubarb is a vegetable, but it has acquired fame in recipes associated with fruits. Rhubarb is called the "pie plant" because its satin stalks are used in pies and tarts, either alone or in combination with fruits, particularly fresh strawberries.

Rhubarb is one of the few produce commodities which

isn't good raw. It needs to be cooked and sweetened to bring out its best qualities.

Only the stalks of rhubarb are eaten. The elephant ear-shaped leaves contain oxalic acid which is poisonous. Most produce retailers remove the leaves from the stalks, but in case they are still attached, remember to discard them.

AVAILABILITY: January through June, with peak supplies in May and June.

SELECTION AND STORAGE: Look for fresh, firm, crisp stalks of medium size. Avoid flabby stalks. The rhubarb's color might not always be ruby red. Varieties grown in different soils can be light pink or even green. Although these types may not be colorful, they still have a rich flavor.

Wrap rhubarb in plastic and refrigerate; it can be kept a week or more.

PREPARATION: Discard any leaves and trim the ends, then slice.

SERVING SUGGESTIONS: Rhubarb can be cooked and sweetened for sauces, combined in sauces with fresh strawberries, or made into pies, tarts, cobblers, jams, or combined with other fruits into a refreshing punch.

NUTRITION INFORMATION: One cup diced rhubarb has vitamin C, potassium, and other nutrients; is low in sodium; and contains 29 calories.

RHUBARB SAUCE

2 pounds fresh rhubarb   ¹/₄ teaspoon ground
1 cup sugar   cinnamon
¹/₄ cup water

Wash rhubarb and trim the ends. Cut rhubarb into ³/₄-inch
pieces. In a large saucepan, combine rhubarb and sugar. Let the
mixture stand for about 10 minutes. Add the water and bring to a
boil, then reduce heat and simmer until tender. Taste for sweetness, adding more sugar and/or cinammon, if desired. Serve
warm or chilled.

MAKES 4 CUPS

* Microwave version: Prepare rhubarb for cooking. Place rhubarb and water in a 1¹/₂-
quart microwaveable dish. Cover and cook on high power 7–9 minutes or until tender,
stirring halfway through cooking. Remove and drain. Place in a food processor. Add
sugar and cinnamon, if desired; purée until smooth.

RHUBARB AND STRAWBERRY SAUCE

³/₄ pound fresh rhubarb   ¹/₂ cup sugar
2 cups sliced fresh
    strawberries

Wash the rhubarb and trim the ends. Cut the rhubarb into ³/₄-inch
pieces. Hull and slice the strawberries. Combine both with the
sugar in a large saucepan and let stand for about 10 minutes.
Cook the mixture over medium heat until tender. Remove from
heat. Cover and chill.

MAKES ABOUT 3 CUPS

RHUBARB STREUSEL

1 cup uncooked rolled oats
1 cup firmly packed brown
  sugar
²/3 cup plus 2 tablespoons
  all-purpose flour
¹/2 cup margarine or butter

1¹/2 pounds fresh rhubarb
²/3 cup sugar
2 tablespoons fresh
  orange juice
Vanilla ice cream or
  frozen yogurt (optional)

In a large mixing bowl combine the oats, brown sugar, and ²/3 cup flour. Cut in margarine or butter using a pastry blender or 2 knives scissor-fashion, until crumbly. Set the mixture aside.

Wash the rhubarb and trim the ends. Cut rhubarb into 1-inch pieces. Place rhubarb in an 8-inch-square baking dish. Add sugar, remaining 2 tablespoons flour, and orange juice. Toss rhubarb to coat with the mixture.

Sprinkle the oats and sugar mixture over the rhubarb. Bake in preheated 350° F oven for 40–45 minutes, or until rhubarb is tender. Serve warm, with ice cream or frozen yogurt, if desired.

MAKES 6 TO 8 SERVINGS

RHUBARB RIBBON CHEESECAKE

Sweetened rhubarb is layered with a rich and creamy cheesecake.

Graham Cracker Crust
(recipe follows)
1 pound fresh rhubarb
1 cup sugar, divided
2 tablespoons flour
11 ounces cream cheese, softened

2 eggs
1 1/2 teaspoons vanilla extract, divided
3/4 cup dairy sour cream
3 tablespoons confectioners sugar

Prepare Graham Cracker Crust and set aside.

Wash rhubarb and trim the ends. Cut rhubarb into 1-inch pieces. In a medium saucepan, combine rhubarb and 1/2 cup sugar. Cover and simmer over medium heat for about 5 minutes, or until nearly tender. Remove from heat. Stir in flour and mix to blend. Pour rhubarb mixture into the prepared crust. Bake in preheated 350° F oven for 10 minutes.

In a mixing bowl, beat the cream cheese until fluffy. Add eggs, one at a time, and beat well to blend. Gradually beat in remaining 1/2 cup sugar; add 1 teaspoon vanilla and mix well. Pour cheese mixture over the rhubarb and bake at 350° F for 35 minutes. Remove from oven and prepare sour cream topping.

In a small bowl, mix together the sour cream, confectioners sugar, and remaining 1/2 teaspoon vanilla; blend well. Top the cheesecake with the sour cream mixture. Return cheesecake to oven and bake for 5 minutes more. Cool and refrigerate for at least 4 hours.

MAKES ONE 9-INCH PIE

GRAHAM CRACKER CRUST

1 1/2 cups graham cracker
  crumbs
1/4 cup granulated sugar

6 tablespoons margarine or
  butter, melted

Mix the ingredients together and firmly press into a 9-inch spring-form pan or pie plate.

STRAWBERRY-RHUBARB COBBLER

COBBLER BISCUIT DOUGH

1 cup sifted all-purpose
  flour
2 tablespoons sugar
1 1/2 teaspoons baking
  powder

1 teaspoon grated orange
  peel
4 tablespoons margarine or
  butter, chilled
1/2 cup milk

FRUIT FILLING

1 pound fresh rhubarb
2/3 cup sugar
1 tablespoon cornstarch
1 tablespoon fresh orange
  juice
1 pint fresh strawberries
  (about 1 pound)

1 teaspoon ground cinnamon
Sweetened whipped cream,
  vanilla ice cream, or frozen
  yogurt

In a large mixing bowl, combine the flour, sugar, baking powder, and orange peel. Cut in the margarine or butter until the mixture resembles coarse crumbs. Stir in the milk all at once and mix just until flour is moistened. Set mixture aside.

Wash rhubarb and trim ends. Cut rhubarb into ³/₄-inch pieces and place in a medium saucepan. Combine the sugar, cornstarch, and orange juice in the same pan. Allow the mixture to stand for about 10 minutes. Bring the mixture to a boil, reduce heat, and cook for 2–3 minutes. Remove from heat.

Hull and slice the strawberries. Stir strawberries and cinnamon into rhubarb mixture. Spoon the fruit into a buttered 8-inch-square baking dish. Spread the dough thoroughly over the hot fruit filling. Bake in preheated 425° F oven for 20–25 minutes, until the dough is golden. Serve the cobbler warm with sweetened whipped cream, vanilla ice cream, or frozen yogurt.

MAKES 6 SERVINGS

RHUBARB LATTICE PIE

1¹/₄ pounds fresh rhubarb
1¹/₄ cups plus 1 tablespoon
sugar
¹/₄ cup all-purpose flour
1 tablespoon water
¹/₂ teaspoon ground
cinnamon

Pie Pastry for 9-inch,
double-crust pie (recipe
follows)
1¹/₂ tablespoons margarine
or butter

Wash the rhubarb and trim the ends. Cut the rhubarb into ³/₄-inch lengths and measure 4 cups. In a large bowl combine rhubarb, 1¹/₄ cups sugar, the flour, water, and cinnamon. Set rhubarb aside for about 10 minutes.

Prepare the pastry. Roll out half of the pastry on a floured surface and place in a 9-inch pie plate. Spoon rhubarb mixture into the pastry. Dot the top with the margarine or butter.

Roll out remaining pastry to a round $^1/_8$-inch thick, and cut into $^1/_2$-inch-wide strips. To form the lattice, place half the strips $^3/_4$-inch apart across the top of the pie, folding back every other strip halfway. Lay a strip across the unfolded strips from front to back. Unfold the strips, folding back the alternating strips. Continue making the lattice across half the pie, then repeat the process for the other half. Lightly moisten the ends of the strips and press strips firmly to the pie edge. Trim the strips even with the edge of the pie plate. Press the dough around the edge with a fork. Sprinkle remaining 1 tablespoon sugar over the lattice top. Bake in a preheated 450° F oven for 10 minutes. Reduce the temperature to 350° F and bake for about 40 minutes longer, or until pastry is golden brown.

MAKES ONE 9-INCH PIE

PIE PASTRY

2 cups sifted all-purpose
   flour
$^1/_2$ teaspoon salt

$^2/_3$ cup chilled shortening
2 tablespoons chilled butter
4 tablespoons cold water

In a medium mixing bowl, combine the flour and salt. Cut half the shortening and half the butter into the flour mixture, using a pastry blender. Add remaining shortening and butter and mix, still using the pastry blender, until the dough pieces are about the size of peas. Sprinkle the dough with cold water and blend lightly. Gather the dough into 2 balls. If dough is to be stored in the refrigerator, cover with plastic wrap. Remove from refrigerator at least 1 hour before rolling out.

MAKES ENOUGH PASTRY FOR 1 9-INCH, DOUBLE-CRUST PIE OR 2 SINGLE-CRUST TARTS

SPRINGTIME PUNCH

1 1/2 pounds fresh rhubarb
1 quart water
1 1/3 cups sugar

6 juice oranges
4 lemons

Wash the rhubarb and trim the ends. Cut rhubarb into 1-inch pieces. Place rhubarb in a large saucepan and add the water. Bring to a boil, cover, and simmer for 10 minutes. Remove from heat and allow to cool for about 15 minutes. Pour the rhubarb into a sieve set over a bowl and reserve the juice. Place the juice in a 2-quart pitcher. Add sugar to the juice and stir until dissolved.

Cut the oranges and lemons into halves. Using a juicer, extract 2 cups orange juice and 1 cup lemon juice. Pour the lemon and orange juices into the pitcher and stir to blend. Serve over ice.

MAKES ABOUT 2 QUARTS

SNOW PEAS AND SUGAR SNAP PEAS

Unlike the English pea, or shelling pea, which is valued for its sweet, succulent seeds, the snow pea is valued for its edible pod. The sugar snap pea combines the best qualities of both the English pea and the snow pea, plump peas enveloped within a crisp, tender edible pod.

The delicate-tasting snow pea, or Chinese pea pod, is popular in Oriental cuisine. However, edible pea pods actually originated in Europe and were introduced into Asia, becoming immediately popular with the Chinese.

Sugar snap peas, a cross between a thick-podded green pea and a snow pea, became a vegetable classic almost instantly from its creation in the late 1970s. They became popular with home gardens during the early 1980s, and that success cultivated commercial interest in the sugar snap.

AVAILABILITY: Snow peas are available year round; sugar snap peas are mainly on the market February to September.

SELECTION AND STORAGE: Select fresh green pods. Snow peas should be thin and flexible, while sugar snaps should have crisp pods. Both varieties are perishable. Keep them refrigerated in plastic.

PREPARATION: With the exception of the stringless sugar snap variety, other sugar snaps and snow peas require stringing. Snap the stem without severing the string and pull the stem down the seam. For snow peas, you may have to string both sides.

Both edible pod varieties may be eaten raw, but blanching brings out the vivid green color and heightens their sweet flavor. Cook in boiling water for less than 1 minute, drain, then plunge into ice water until chilled.

COOKING METHODS: Proper cooking is essential for retaining the crispness of edible-pod peas. Whichever cooking method is selected keep cooking time brief.

To stir-fry: Heat 1 tablespoon vegetable oil in a skillet and sauté peas 1 to 2 minutes or just until crisp-tender. Peas can also be sautéed in a little butter or margarine, instead of the oil, then add a few teaspoons of water, cover, and cook about 30 seconds longer.

To steam: Arrange peas in a steam basket, cover, and cook 3 to 4 minutes or until crisp-tender.

TO MICROWAVE: For 1 pound edible-pod peas, place peas in a 2-quart microwaveable baking dish. Add a little water, cover, and microcook on high power 4 to 5 minutes, stirring halfway through cooking. Allow to stand, covered for a few minutes longer.

SERVING SUGGESTIONS:

- Top hot cooked pea pods with margarine or butter and season with fresh herbs, such as mint, basil, or tarragon.

- Briefly blanch pods, chill, and serve plain as a crudité, or pipe spiced cream cheese into the pods.
- Season pods with lemon, ginger, or scallions.
- Blanch, chill, and serve with a vinaigrette.
- Add to stir-fry combinations the last few minutes of cooking.

NUTRITION INFORMATION: Snow peas are an excellent source of vitamin C, and provide vitamin A, potassium, and fiber. A 3½-ounce serving of raw snow peas contains about 42 calories; less when cooked. Snow peas and sugar snaps are low in sodium.

LEMON-GINGER SHRIMP, PENNE, AND PEA POD SALAD

1¼ pounds large shrimp
2 lemons
¼ cup white wine vinegar
2 tablespoons honey
1½ tablespoons reduced-sodium soy sauce
1½ tablespoons chopped fresh gingerroot
1 garlic clove, minced
Dash of cayenne pepper
10 ounces dry penne pasta (3 cups)
2 tablespoons sesame oil
6 ounces fresh snow peas or sugar snaps
1 medium red bell pepper
4 scallions

Peel and devein the shrimp; set aside. Grate the peel from two lemons; reserve. Juice lemons and measure 3 tablespoons juice. Place juice in a medium saucepan. Add the vinegar, honey, soy sauce, ginger, garlic, and cayenne; stir until well-blended. Add shrimp. Bring the mixture to a boil, cover, and remove from heat. Let stand about 10–12 minutes, stirring occasionally until shrimp are opaque in center. Using a slotted spoon, lift shrimp from liquid, reserving cooking liquid; cover and refrigerate shrimp.

Meanwhile, bring 3 quarts water to a boil in a large kettle. Add penne, stir, and cook uncovered for about 12–15 minutes, or cook according to package directions. Drain, rinse with cold water, and drain again. Place penne in a 3-quart bowl. Add sesame oil and lemon peel to reserved cooking liquid; pour over penne and toss. Chill penne mixture while preparing vegetables. (If preparing a day in advance, shrimp can be added to penne mixture at this point and refrigerated. Add vegetables a few hours before serving.)

Trim the pea pods and remove the strings, if any. Blanch pea pods and cook 1 minute. Drain, then plunge pea pods into ice water. Remove seeds and membrane from the pepper; dice pepper. Chop scallions. Drain pea pods. Add shrimp and all vegetables to penne mixture; toss to coat. Cover and chill at least 1 hour or more for the shrimp and pasta to absorb lemon-ginger mixture.

MAKES 4 TO 5 SERVINGS

BEEF WITH SNOW PEAS AND SHIITAKE MUSHROOMS

1 pound lean boneless beef (sirloin or flank steak)

2 garlic cloves

1 tablespoon dry sherry

1 tablespoon hoisin sauce

1 tablespoon vegetable oil

1 tablespoon sesame oil

1 tablespoon cornstarch

1/2 pound fresh snow peas or sugar snap peas

1/4 pound fresh shiitake mushrooms

1 medium onion

4 tablespoons peanut oil, divided

1 1/2 tablespoons reduced-sodium soy sauce

1 teaspoon sugar

Trim fat from beef. Slice the beef across the grain into thin strips. Peel and mince the garlic. Place beef and garlic in a shallow bowl. Combine the sherry, hoisin sauce, vegetable oil, sesame oil, and cornstarch; stir together and pour over the meat. Cover and refrigerate at least 1 hour.

Trim snow peas or sugar snaps, removing any strings. Wipe mushrooms with a damp cloth; thinly slice stems and caps. Peel and cut onion into thin slices.

Heat 2 tablespoons peanut oil in a large skillet or wok. Add pea pods; stir-fry 1 minute; add mushrooms and stir-fry 1 more minute. Remove vegetables from skillet; set aside. Heat remaining 2 tablespoons oil. Add beef and any marinade; stir-fry 2–3 minutes or until beef is browned. Add onion, soy sauce, and sugar; stir-fry 1 minute. Return pea pods and mushrooms to skillet and toss beef and vegetables just to heat through.

MAKES 4 SERVINGS

SPAGHETTI SQUASH

The exact origin of spaghetti squash, or vegetable spa-ghetti, is a mystery, but the Japanese perfected it during the twentieth century. Spaghetti squash is an edible gourd which is a member of the Cucurbitaceae *family, but it is*

indeed a novel relative—when cooked, its flesh is transformed into golden, spaghettilike strands.

It has a sweet, mild flavor, with a distinctively crunchy texture. The bland strands are perfect for seasoning or cradling flavorful sauces.

Spaghetti squash is oval-shaped with a smooth skin ranging in color from pale to bright yellow or orange. It generally weighs about 2–4 pounds.

AVAILABILITY: Year round.

SELECTION AND STORAGE: Look for squash with hard shells. Avoid any which are green, indicating immaturity. Store squash at room temperature in a cool, dry place. If purchased in good condition, squash will keep several weeks.

PREPARATION: Spaghetti squash can be prepared by several cooking methods. Once the squash is cooked, cut into halves, scoop out and discard the seeds, then fluff out all the strands with a fork, removing them all until only the shell remains.

To bake: Pierce the squash with a fork in several places, then place in a shallow baking pan. Bake at 375° F about 45 minutes or more depending on size.

To boil: Cook whole in a large pot of boiling water for 25–30 minutes, or until tender.

To microwave: Pierce the shell in several places, then cook on high power 12–15 minutes, rotating halfway through cooking.

To steam: Halve the squash and scoop out the seeds. Cut the squash into halves again and place on a steamer rack. Cover and cook over boiling water 20–30 minutes, or until tender.

Serving Suggestions:

- Top cooked squash with a marinara or white clam sauce.
- Toss cooked strands with margarine or butter, grated Parmesan cheese, and fresh herbs.
- Chill cooked strands and toss with a vinaigrette.
- Top cooked squash with a fresh vegetable mélange.

Nutrition Information: A 1-cup serving provides vitamins A and C, fiber, and potassium; is low in sodium; and has just 45 calories.

SPAGHETTI SQUASH WITH EGGPLANT TOPPING

1 spaghetti squash, about 3 pounds
1 eggplant, about 2 pounds
1/2 teaspoon salt
1 garlic clove
4–5 tablespoons olive oil

1 teaspoon dried basil
1/2 teaspoon dried oregano
3 tablespoons margarine or butter
3/4 cup freshly grated Parmesan cheese
Fresh parsley sprigs

Prepare the squash according to one of the methods outlined on page 251. Set the squash aside.

Peel eggplant and cut into 1/2-inch cubes; there should be 4–5 cups. Sprinkle the cubes with salt and let stand for 15–20 minutes. Peel and mince the garlic. Heat 4 tablespoons oil in a large skillet. Add the eggplant, garlic, and herbs. Sauté over medium heat for 8–10 minutes, or until the eggplant is tender, adding more oil if needed.

Remove the seeds and fibrous strands from the cooked squash.

Loosen squash strands with a fork, remove from the shell, and heap on a serving platter. Melt the margarine or butter and drizzle over squash. Drain excess oil from the eggplant mixture and place eggplant on squash. Sprinkle with the cheese and garnish with parsley.

MAKES 4 MAIN-DISH SERVINGS

FRESH VEGETABLE PRIMAVERA

1 spaghetti squash, about 3 pounds
1 pound fresh broccoli
1 large onion
1 medium red bell pepper
1 garlic clove
1/2 pound fresh mushrooms
1 large tomato

3 tablespoons vegetable oil
1 tablespoon minced fresh basil or 1 teaspoon dried basil
1/2 teaspoon salt
Pinch of black pepper
1/2 cup freshly grated Parmesan cheese

Prepare spaghetti squash by one of the methods outlined on page 251. Remove from heat and set aside to cool slightly.

Prepare vegetables for cooking. Trim broccoli and cut into florets. Peel and slice onion. Remove seeds and membrane from peppers; slice pepper. Peel and mince garlic. Wipe mushrooms with a damp cloth, trim stems, and slice mushrooms. Blanch, peel, and dice tomato.

Heat oil in a large skillet or wok. Add broccoli, onion, red or green pepper, garlic, basil, and seasonings; sauté over medium-high heat for 5 minutes. Add mushrooms and tomato and continue cooking until vegetables are tender.

Cut squash into halves and remove seeds and fibrous strands surrounding seeds. Loosen squash strands with a fork and heap on a serving platter. Top with vegetable mixture. Sprinkle with cheese.

MAKES 4 OR 5 MAIN-DISH SERVINGS

$\mathcal{S}$PROUTS

There are several varieties of sprouts. Alfalfa and mung bean sprouts are the most available, but there are a number of seeds and beans for adding crunchy texture and extra flavor to salads, sandwiches, and other dishes. Some of these include radish seeds, wheat berries, lentils, sunflower seeds, mustard cress, fennel seeds, and coriander.

Mung bean sprouts and alfalfa sprouts are mild while other sprout varieties can be peppery and hot. With the exception of mung bean sprouts, most are served raw. Mung bean sprouts have been cultivated for thousands of years and are a familiar ingredient in stir-fry recipes.

AVAILABILITY: Year round.

SELECTION AND STORAGE: Look for fresh-looking sprouts. Refrigerate unwashed in plastic and use within a few days.

PREPARATION: Rinse sprouts before serving. If serving them raw, chill in ice water—refreshing them first in ice water adds extra crispness—then drain well. There's no need to remove the loose hulls or little roots.

When cooking mung bean or other sprouts, keep cooking time very brief to retain their crispness.

SERVING SUGGESTIONS:

- Add bean sprouts to stir-frys, omelets, and fried rice.
- Tuck raw sprouts into sandwiches or add to salads.
- Season cooked sprouts with soy sauce, garlic, or ginger.

NUTRITION INFORMATION: A 1-cup serving of raw mung bean sprouts contains 37 calories and provides vitamin C, fiber, and a very small amount of protein. A 2-ounce serving of alfalfa sprouts contains about 20 calories and provides vitamin A and fiber.

SESAME RICE AND SPROUT SAUTÉ

2 cups hot, steamed, unsalted rice

3 tablespoons sesame seeds

2 garlic cloves

4 scallions

2 cups fresh bean sprouts

1 tablespoon peanut oil

1 tablespoon reduced-sodium soy sauce

1 tablespoon oyster sauce

Set cooked rice aside. Heat a large skillet over medium heat. Add sesame seeds and stir until golden, about 1½–2 minutes. Transfer seeds to a blender and whirl briefly or crush seeds coarsely with a mortar and pestle.

Peel and mince garlic. Thinly slice scallions. Rinse sprouts and pat dry. Heat oil in skillet. Add garlic, scallions, and sesame seeds; stir-fry 1 minute. Add bean sprouts and sauté 1 minute. Add rice, soy sauce, and oyster sauce, and stir to combine just enough to heat through. Serve hot.

MAKES 4 SERVINGS

FRIED RICE

2 cups cooked, unsalted rice
3 tablespoons peanut oil
3/4 cup chopped celery
1 egg
2 cups fresh bean sprouts
3/4 cup chopped scallions

1/2 cup diced cooked shrimp, pork, or chicken
2–3 tablespoons reduced-sodium soy sauce
Black pepper

Set cooked rice aside. In a large skillet or wok, heat the oil. Add the celery and sauté over medium heat for 2 minutes. Add the egg and cook until the egg is set. In the same skillet, combine the rice, bean sprouts, scallions, and shrimp or meat. Sauté the mixture for 3 to 4 minutes. Add soy sauce and pepper to taste and mix well. Serve hot.

MAKES 3 TO 4 MAIN-DISH SERVINGS OR 6 SIDE-DISH SERVINGS

TAMARILLO

The shiny, egg-shaped tamarillo, also known as the tree tomato, is a stunning fruit. Its satinlike skin is either a brilliant purplish-red or orangish-yellow. Inside the plum-textured flesh is yellowish-orange with a swirl of edible red seeds.

The tamarillo originated in South America and is now cultivated throughout Central and South America, the Caribbean, Asia, Australia, and New Zealand, the country which supplies most of the fruit for the United States.

Like the tomato, the tamarillo has an identity problem—consumers aren't sure if they should prepare it as a fruit or vegetable. Its flavor is reminiscent of plums, tomatoes, or a tart apple, but is not a good out-of-hand fruit for its skin is acrid and its flesh is slightly bitter. This glossy fruit requires sweetening and cooking to be at its fullest and most flavorful. Hence, the tamarillo is best when cooked into a sauce, simmered in a syrup or other preparations which will tame its tart taste and bring out its finest qualities.

AVAILABILITY: Early spring through fall, with peak supplies May through August.

SELECTION AND STORAGE: Select firm fruit. The orange-yellow varieties tend to be sweeter than the scarlet varieties. Keep fruit at room temperature until it yields slightly to gentle pressure and becomes fragrant. Then use or refrigerate. Ripe fruit can be refrigerated for several weeks. About 4 or 5 fruit equals a pound.

PREPARATION: Peeling the fruit is essential either with a vegetable peeler or by plunging fruit into a pot of boiling water for 30–60 seconds, cooling in ice water, then slipping off skins. Handle red fruits carefully to avoid stains left by the flesh.

SERVING SUGGESTIONS:

- Bake fruit in a cinnamon-spiced syrup at 350° F for about 30 minutes or until the skin can be pulled off easily. Then stir rum into the syrup. Serve warm or spoon over vanilla frozen yogurt or coffee ice cream.
- Use in chutneys, relishes, and sauces.
- Peel, cut lengthwise into halves, then sauté and season for a side dish.
- Add peeled and sweetened fruit to fruit salads.

NUTRITION INFORMATION: According to the New Zealand Tamarillo Growers Association, tamarillos provide fiber and vitamins A and C. The red variety has 36 calories per $3^1/_2$ ounces while the yellow variety has 27 calories.

SWEETPOTATOES WITH TAMARILLO-ORANGE SAUCE

4 *medium sweetpotatoes*   *¹/₃ cup sugar*
¹/₄ cup water   2 *teaspoons cornstarch*
³/₄ pound tamarillos (about   *Dash ground cayenne*
    5)   *pepper*
¹/₃ cup fresh orange juice   *Shredded coconut*

Wash and peel sweetpotatoes; cut into ¹/₂-inch thick slices. Combine sweetpotatoes and water in a 2-quart microwaveable casserole. Cover and microwave on high power for 7–8 minutes or until soft. Remove from oven; drain and set aside.

Cover tamarillos with boiling water; let stand 1 minute. Drain and peel, starting with stem end. Cut crosswise into ¹/₂-inch rounds; cut each round into quarters. Set aside.

In a medium microwaveable bowl, combine orange juice, sugar, and cornstarch. Cover with wax paper and cook on high power 1¹/₂–2 minutes or until thickened, stirring halfway through cooking. Stir in tamarillos and pepper; gently toss to coat thoroughly. Cover and microwave on high power about 1 minute or just until tamarillos are warmed through. Remove from oven. Spoon over sweetpotatoes. Garnish with coconut.

MAKES 4 SERVINGS

SPICED TAMARILLO TOPPING

4 tamarillos
1/3 cup sugar
1/2 teaspoon ground
   cinnamon

3 tablespoons peach brandy

Pour boiling water over tamarillos; let stand 1 minute. Drain and peel from stem end. Slice tamarillos in half lengthwise, then crosswise into 1/4-inch half-rounds. Combine with sugar, cinnamon, and brandy in a saucepan. Cook over medium heat until mixture thickens slightly, about 15 minutes. Serve warm or cold over angel food cake, ice cream, or frozen yogurt.

MAKES 1 CUP

GRILLED SWORDFISH WITH CHUNKY SWEET-AND-SOUR SAUCE

2 tamarillos
1/2 cup diced fresh pineapple
1/4 cup chopped scallions
1 garlic clove, minced
1/2 cup pineapple juice
1/2 cup dry white wine
1/4 cup firmly packed brown
   sugar
2 tablespoons white wine
   vinegar

4 teaspoons cornstarch
1 tablespoon ketchup
2 tablespoons reduced-
   sodium soy sauce
1 tablespoon vegetable oil
4 swordfish steaks, each
   about 6–8 ounces

Peel and cut tamarillos in half lengthwise; cut crosswise into ¼-inch slices. Prepare pineapple and vegetables for cooking; set aside.

In a cup, combine pineapple juice, wine, brown sugar, vinegar, cornstarch, ketchup, and soy sauce; stir to combine.

In a medium saucepan, heat oil; add garlic and sauté 30 seconds over medium heat. Add fruit and vegetables and pour in reserved juice mixture. Cook uncovered for about 5–7 minutes or just until vegetables are crisp-tender.

Place swordfish over hot grill. Cook swordfish about 10 minutes or until done, turning once.

Remove swordfish from grill and spoon about ½ cup sauce over each steak. Serve immediately.

MAKES 4 SERVINGS

*T*AMARIND

The flattened tamarind (tam' -ə-rind) pods, resembling enlarged pole beans in shape, envelop a sticky datelike pulp. The pulp has an acidic flavor with hints of lemon and dried apricot. The tamarind is a familiar seasoning ingredient to Asian cooks for meats, chutneys, and sauces. In fact,

*tamarind is one of the flavoring contributions in Worces-
tershire sauce.*

*Tamarind is believed to be native to tropical Africa and
southern Asia. Marco Polo is credited with introducing
tamarind to Europe in the late-thirteenth century. Centuries
later, Spanish and Portuguese explorers brought the tamarind to the New World.*

*The pods range from 2–8 inches long. Immature pods
are greenish-brown turning to a rusty-brown as they mature.
Tamarinds can be used either when the pods are green and
immature or when the shell pod has turned brown and
brittle.*

AVAILABILITY: Year round.

SELECTION AND STORAGE: Pods may be cracked, but
shouldn't be crumbled or moldy. They can be wrapped in plastic
and kept at room temperature or refrigerated. Tamarinds are
great keepers and can be stored for months.

PREPARATION: Crack and peel the pods from the pulp with
your fingers and remove any long fibers or strings. The pulp can
be eaten raw like fruit leather, but is better known for making a
distinctively flavored concentrate which can be used in marinades
or sauces for meats, poultry and seafood, chutneys, curries, and
beverages.

For 1½ cups concentrate, peel ¼ pound tamarinds and soak
the pulp in 1½ cups hot water for several hours, then strain the
pulp through a sieve into a bowl, pressing out the liquid.

SERVING SUGGESTIONS: Tamarinds are primarily used for
flavoring as listed above. The strained liquid can be sweetened
with sugar, flavored with lemon, ginger, or cardamon, and used as

the base for drinks, syrups, and other recipes. In India, tamarinds are used in lentil, vegetable, and bean recipes. Oriental cooks mix the grated pulp from green tamarinds with chili peppers for a salad.

NUTRITION INFORMATION: One fruit provides potassium, iron, phosphorous, and calcium, and is about 5 calories.

BROILED TAMARIND MAHI MAHI

6 (3-inch) tamarind pods
1 cup boiling water
1 jalapeño pepper
1 tablespoon minced fresh
   ginger
1 garlic clove, minced
1/2 teaspoon curry powder
1/4 teaspoon salt
4 mahi mahi fillets, each
   about 8 ounces

Crack open tamarind shells; peel back from seeds and pulp. Peel off the long fibers and cut pulp away from seeds; discard seeds. Soak pulp in the water for 2 hours. Press out all juice from pulp. Strain mixture into a bowl.

Remove seeds and membrane from pepper; chop pepper and measure 1 tablespoon. In a shallow dish, combine pepper, strained tamarind mixture, ginger, garlic, curry powder, and salt. Add fillets, turning to coat with mixture. Cover and refrigerate at least 1 hour.

Drain fillets, reserving marinade. Bring marinade to a boil. Keep warm while cooking fish.

Lightly coat the rack of a broiler pan with a nonstick cooking spray and place fillets on rack. Place under broiler and broil about 8–10 minutes or just until fish flakes easily when tested with a fork, basting occasionally with marinade. Serve with remaining marinade.

MAKES 4 SERVINGS

TROPICAL TEA

$^1/_2$ pound tamarind pods
3 cups boiling water
2 cinnamon-spice tea bags
2 (6$^1/_2$-ounce) bottles
   sparkling mineral water,
   chilled

Ice cubes
Lemon wedges
Ground cinnamon

Crack open tamarind shells; peel back from seeds and pulp. Peel off the long strings or fibers and cut the pulp away from the seeds. Discard seeds. Soak pulp in the water for 2 hours. Press out all juice from pulp. Strain mixture into a glass jar; add tea bags. Cover tightly and shake vigorously. Chill at least 8 hours.

Strain mixture into a pitcher; discard tea bags. Gently stir mineral water into tea mixture. Pour into glasses over ice cubes. If desired, dip edges of lemon wedges into cinnamon and place on rims of serving glasses.

MAKES 4 SERVINGS

Taro

There are many different varieties of the Arum family that make classification difficult for the tropical, tuber-bearing plant known as taro, dasheen, eddo, tannia, cocoyam, among many others. Taro has been cultivated for 4,000–7,000 years, and has acquired many names during its long history and journey around the world. Taro is native to Southeast Asia, having been brought by traders about 2,500 years ago to Japan, China, and the Mediterranean. About the time of Christ, taro reached the South Pacific, brought by those migrating from Southeast Asia. Centuries later, it arrived in New Zealand and Hawaii.

Taro's skin is cocoa brown with a shaggy, rough texture encircled with distinct rings. The tubers vary in size and shape—some are barrel-shaped while others are elongated or kidney-shaped and may have little corms or pinkish sprouts. Underneath the hairy skin is a flesh ranging from pristine white, cream, lavender-gray, or even dotted with brownish specks. However, during cooking even the whitest flesh turns grayish or a pale violet.

Taro has a sweet, nutty flavor reminiscent of artichoke hearts, Jerusalem artichokes, or chestnuts.

AVAILABILITY: Year round.

SELECTION AND STORAGE: Choose firm tubers without any signs of decay or shriveling. Sometimes taro is cut to show its moist, fresh flesh which is another sign of quality. Corms less than 6–7 ounces are moist and excellent for steaming or boiling whole. Larger tubers are well-suited for other cooking techniques, particularly those where a drier texture is preferred.

At home, keep taro in a cool, dry, well-ventilated area, the same as for potatoes, sweetpotatoes, and winter squash—do not refrigerate until after cooking. Although it looks rugged, taro is best if used within a few days.

PREPARATION: Taro requires cooking and should never be eaten raw because some varieties contain calcium oxalate which can cause irritation to the digestive tract. Raw taro can also irritate the skin, so you may want to wear gloves or oil your hands while preparing it. Pare the skin and remove any discolored spots, then plunge into cold water.

Because taro is a dense-textured vegetable, it requires some selective preparation, otherwise a heavy, glutinous texture results. For this reason, unlike other starchy vegetables, taro is not suited simply to boiling or steaming then mashing or puréeing alone. Taro also dries out when baked, so it takes well to sauces or toppings that will enhance and flavor it.

SERVING SUGGESTIONS:

- Fry slices, either by sautéing or deep-frying, and season with herbs and spices.
- Shred taro for vegetable patties or deep-fry for nests to cradle seafood, poultry, or vegetable combinations.
- Purée cooked taro for soups or soufflés.
- Add chunks to soups or stews.

NUTRITION INFORMATION: Taro provides potassium, iron, fiber, and other nutrients; is low in sodium; and has about 120 calories per 3½-ounce serving.

SPICY MEXICAN CHIPS

1 taro root, about 12 ounces   *½ teaspoon ground cumin*
Vegetable oil   *½ teaspoon salt*
1 teaspoon chili powder

Peel taro and cut in half lengthwise. Use a vegetable peeler to slice paper-thin rounds.

Pour oil into a large skillet to a depth of ¾ inch. Heat oil to a temperature of about 365° F on a candy/deep-fry thermometer. Cook until crisp and browned. Drain on paper towels.

Combine remaining ingredients and sprinkle on taro root while still warm.

MAKES 3 TO 4 SERVINGS

$\mathcal{T}$OMATILLO

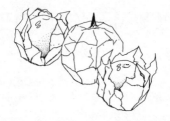

With American palates now thoroughly tantalized by Mexican and Tex-Mex cuisine, the traditional produce items used in preparing these dishes are quickly becoming produce staples. One such commodity is the tart, snappy-tasting tomatillo (pronounced to-ma-teé-o).

Tomatillos resemble cherry tomatoes encased in papery-green or tan husks. Underneath the easily peeled parchment husk is a small, waxy fruit. They are usually green, but if ripened fully on the vine, they might be yellow or tinged with purple.

Tomatillos are particularly good in salsas and sauces, such as salsa verde, the spicy green sauce used to enliven many Southwestern and Mexican dishes. Tomatillos are generally cooked to develop their flavor and soften their flesh, but can also be eaten raw, prepared in salsas, gazpachos, or guacamole.

AVAILABILITY: Year round.

SELECTION AND STORAGE: Choose fresh-looking tomatillos with firm, dry, close-fitting husks. Tomatillos should feel firm to the touch, without the same "give" of tomatoes. Tomatillos keep best refrigerated in their husks in a paper bag–lined basket or dish. If purchased in good condition, they should keep several weeks in the refrigerator.

PREPARATION: Peel the husks and thoroughly wash the fruit of its sticky residue and remove the core. Tomatillos can be simmered or roasted until tender. Poaching tomatillos yields a saucier result, while roasting produces a drier type of sauce.

To poach, place husked tomatillos in a saucepan with enough water to cover and cook until tender. Cooking time will vary according to the size of the fruit.

Tomatillos can be roasted either with their husks on or without. Bake tomatillos at 500° F in an ungreased dish about 10–15 minutes. Remove and allow to cool, then twist off husks, if still attached, and rinse.

SERVING SUGGESTIONS:

- Simmer with onions, garlic, chili peppers, and other ingredients for flavorful sauces.
- Serve raw, finely chopped in gazpachos, guacamole, and salsas.

NUTRITION INFORMATION: Tomatillos provide vitamins A and C, and 100 calories per cup.

HUEVOS RANCHEROS IN PATTY SHELLS

6 frozen patty shells
2 large red bell peppers
2 large onions
2 garlic cloves
3 tablespoons vegetable oil
1 pound fresh tomatillos
1/2 to 3/4 cup water
2 teaspoons chili powder

1 tablespoon minced fresh
   oregano or 3/4 teaspoon
   dried oregano
1/2 teaspoon salt
1/4 teaspoon black pepper
Butter
6 poached eggs

Bake patty shells according to package instructions. While shells are baking, prepare the sauce. Remove seeds and membrane from peppers; chop the peppers. Peel and chop the onions. Peel and mince the garlic. In a large skillet, heat the oil. Add the peppers, onions, and garlic. Sauté over medium heat for about 5 minutes.

Remove the husks and cores from the tomatillos; rinse them and chop. Add tomatillos, 1/2 cup water, the chili powder, oregano, and seasonings to the sautéed vegetables. Simmer for 10–15 minutes, adding more water if necessary.

To poach eggs, butter a skillet and pour in about 1 inch of water, enough to cover the eggs. Bring water to a boil, then reduce heat to the simmering point. Break the eggs one at a time into a cup and quickly slip each egg into the water, placing eggs side by side. Cover the skillet and cook eggs for 3–5 minutes, until egg whites are firm. Remove eggs with a slotted spatula and drain well.

Place eggs in baked patty shells. Pour sauce over eggs and serve immediately.

MAKES 6 SERVINGS

MARINATED MEXICAN SALAD

$^1/_2$ *pound fresh tomatillos*
2 *medium tomatoes*
1 *large cucumber*
$^1/_2$ *cup chopped red onion*
$^1/_2$ *cup olive or vegetable oil*

3 *tablespoons red wine*
  vinegar
$^1/_2$ *teaspoon salt*
$^1/_2$ *teaspoon dried basil*
$^1/_8$ *teaspoon black pepper*

Remove husks from tomatillos. Rinse, core, and chop tomatillos and tomatoes. Peel and slice the cucumber. Place all the vegetables in a mixing bowl.

In a screw-top jar, combine the oil, vinegar, salt, basil, and pepper; shake well. Pour the dressing over the vegetables. Cover and refrigerate. Marinate for at least 1 hour before serving.

MAKES 4 SERVINGS

CHICKEN ENCHILADAS VERDE

Tomatillo Sauce (see recipe
  on page 272)
3 *cups coarsely shredded,*
  cooked chicken or turkey
2 *cups shredded Monterey*
  Jack cheese, divided
2 *anaheim chili peppers,*
  roasted, seeded, and diced
1 *teaspoon dried oregano*
  leaves

Salt and freshly ground
  black pepper
Vegetable oil
10 *corn tortillas (6–7-inch*
  diameter)
$^2/_3$ *cup dairy sour cream*
Minced fresh cilantro

Prepare Tomatillo Sauce; set aside. (Sauce can be made a day in advance.)

In a mixing bowl, combine chicken, 1 cup cheese, chilies, and oregano. Season with salt and pepper to taste; set aside.

Heat about $1/4$ cup oil in a medium skillet. Add one tortilla at a time, heating briefly on each side, just until limp; drain on paper towels. Immediately after heating each tortilla, place about $1/3$ cup chicken mixture down center of tortilla. Roll tortilla and place seam side down in a lightly oiled 10-inch by 15-inch baking dish. (You can prepare this a day in advance, cover, and refrigerate until ready to bake.)

Cover enchiladas with foil and bake in a preheated 350° F oven about 10–15 minutes, or until hot in center. Uncover and top with the remaining 1 cup cheese. Return to oven and bake uncovered about 2–3 minutes, just until cheese melts.

Meanwhile, heat Tomatillo Sauce. To serve, spoon about $3/4$ cup Tomatillo Sauce onto a large, rimmed platter or divide among 5 dinner plates. Place enchiladas on sauce. Spoon about 1 table-spoon sour cream over each center, sprinkle with a little minced cilantro, and serve.

MAKES 5 SERVINGS*

* For fewer than 5 servings, prepare the full recipe, but reserve $3/4$ cup sauce per serving and bake only the number of enchiladas needed, reserving the others for baking later.

TOMATILLO SAUCE

3 anaheim chili peppers
2 medium onions
3 large garlic cloves
1 pound fresh tomatillos
2 ounces fresh cilantro (about 2 cups, packed)

2 tablespoons vegetable oil
1 cup chicken stock
2 tablespoons fresh lime juice
1 teaspoon ground cumin
$1/2$ teaspoon salt

Remove seeds and membrane from peppers; slice peppers. Peel and slice onions and garlic. Peel, husk, and remove stems from tomatillos; cut tomatillos into halves. Trim roots from cilantro and discard. Separate cilantro stems and leaves; set both aside.

Heat oil in a medium saucepan. Add peppers, onion, and garlic; sauté over medium heat 4–5 minutes, or until onion is tender. Add tomatillos, cilantro stems (reserve leaves for later), and chicken stock. Cover and cook over medium heat about 15 minutes, or until tomatillos are tender.

Pour half the tomatillo mixture into food processor; add lime juice, reserved cilantro leaves, and cumin. Purée until smooth. Pour mixture into a large bowl. Purée remaining tomatillo mixture; add to bowl. Add salt; stir to combine. Use immediately or refrigerate for later use.

MAKES 4 CUPS

SALSA VERDE

A zesty topping for tacos, tostadas, and other Mexican dishes. Also good over grilled poultry or fish.

$1/2$ pound fresh tomatillos	2 tablespoons minced fresh
1 anaheim or poblano chili	cilantro
pepper	2 tablespoons fresh lime
1 jalapeño pepper	juice
1 garlic clove	$1/4$ teaspoon salt
$1/3$ cup coarsely diced onion	$1/4$ teaspoon ground cumin

Peel, husk, and rinse tomatillos, then core and halve them. Place tomatillos in a small saucepan, cover with water, and bring to a boil. Cook over medium heat 4–6 minutes or until tender.

Meanwhile, seed chilies, remove membrane, and coarsely chop chilies. Peel garlic. In a food processor, combine chilies, garlic, and onion. Drain tomatillos and place in food processor. Add cilantro, lime juice, salt, and cumin. Process until smooth. Serve at room temperature.

MAKES 1 CUP

NOTE: Salsa can be prepared in advance and refrigerated.

CHILLED ASPARAGUS WITH TOMATILLO SALSA

1 pound fresh asparagus
6 ounces tomatillos
1 small tomato
3 tablespoons chopped onion
1 teaspoon minced chili
pepper

2 teaspoons chopped
cilantro
2 teaspoons olive oil
1/4 teaspoon ground cumin
Salt and coarsely ground
black pepper
Lemon or lime wedges

Snap off and discard tough ends of asparagus; peel asparagus. In a large skillet, bring about 1 inch water to a boil over high heat. Add asparagus, cover, and cook over medium-high heat about 4–5 minutes or just until tender. Drain; plunge into ice water. When thoroughly chilled, arrange asparagus on 4 salad plates.

Husk, core, and finely dice tomatillos; measure 3/4 cup. Peel, seed, and chop tomato. In a bowl, combine chopped tomato, tomatillos, onion, chili pepper, cilantro, oil, and cumin. Season with salt and pepper to taste.

Spoon salsa over asparagus. Garnish with wedges of lemon or lime.

MAKES 4 SERVINGS

Timesaver tip: Salsa can be made ahead and just spooned over chilled asparagus at serving time.

$\mathcal{W}$ATER CHESTNUT

The water chestnut has long been cultivated in China. The tropical rushlike aquatic plant grows in shallow waters along marshes and lakes. It bears bulbous or flattened, brown or black tubers prized for their firm white flesh and distinctive nutty flavor. Their crunchy texture is reminiscent of jícama or an apple.

AVAILABILITY: Chinese water chestnuts are available year round in varying volume.

SELECTION AND STORAGE: Look for firm tubers, avoiding any with soft spots or decay. Select shiny specimens, if available, though those with dull skins are fine as long as they're not dried.

Water chestnuts can be stored unwashed in a paper bag and refrigerated up to two weeks. They can be placed in a capped jar and refrigerated for the same length of time. Peeled water chestnuts can be frozen in a resealable container and used as needed.

PREPARATION: Scrub, then peel water chestnuts with a paring knife and slice as desired. They can be eaten either raw or cooked. Water chestnuts retain their crispness after cooking. They are best when prepared in combination with other ingredients.

SERVING SUGGESTIONS:

- Toss into salads, omelets, soups, and stews.
- Add to stir-fry recipes.
- Serve as a crudité.
- Chop and add to ground meats.
- Marinate in teriyaki sauce, wrap in bacon, and broil for a crunchy appetizer.

NUTRITION INFORMATION: A 3¹/₂-ounce half-cup serving of cooked water chestnuts has 50 calories and provides vitamin C, potassium, and other nutrients. Water chestnuts are low in sodium.

SHRIMP WITH ASPARAGUS, SNOW PEAS, AND WATER CHESTNUTS

1 pound raw medium shrimp
1 garlic clove
1 pound fresh asparagus
¹/₂ pound fresh snow peas or sugar snap peas
10 fresh water chestnuts
4 scallions
2 teaspoons cornstarch

³/₄ teaspoon sugar
2 tablespoons dry white wine
1¹/₂ tablespoons reduced-sodium soy sauce
¹/₃ cup chicken stock or broth
3 tablespoons peanut oil

Shell and devein shrimp. Peel and mince garlic. Set aside. Snap off and discard tough ends of asparagus spears; cut spears into 1¹/₂-inch pieces. Trim the snow peas or sugar snaps, removing any strings. Peel water chestnuts and thinly slice them. Thinly slice scallions. Set vegetables aside.

In a cup, combine the cornstarch, sugar, wine, and soy sauce; mix well. Stir in the chicken stock; set aside.

Heat the oil in a wok or large skillet. Add the garlic and shrimp; stir-fry over medium-high heat about 1 minute. Add asparagus and sauté over medium-high heat about 3 minutes. Add snow peas, water chestnuts, and scallions, sautéing 1 minute or just until snow peas are crisp-tender. Stir in the reserved sauce, cooking until the sauce boils and thickens and shrimp is fully cooked.

MAKES 4 SERVINGS

STUFFED MUSHROOMS ORIENTAL

15 large fresh mushrooms
3 tablespoons butter
1/4 pound fresh water
chestnuts

3/4 cup soft bread crumbs
3 tablespoons scallions
2 teaspoons reduced-sodium
soy sauce

Wipe mushrooms with a damp cloth. Remove the stems and chop them, reserving the caps. In a large skillet, melt the butter. Place mushroom caps and chopped stems in skillet and cook over medium heat for about 2 minutes. Turn caps and cook for 1–2 minutes longer. Remove the caps and drain upside down on paper toweling.

Peel and chop the water chestnuts. Mix together the chopped mushroom stems, water chestnuts, bread crumbs, scallions, and soy sauce. Stuff caps with water chestnut mixture. Place on a shallow baking sheet and bake in preheated 350° F oven for 8–10 minutes. Serve immediately.

MAKES 15 STUFFED MUSHROOM CAPS

ᗯHITE SAPOTE

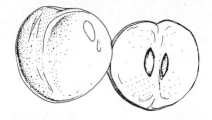

The smooth-textured white sapote (sah-PO-tay), also known as the Mexican custard apple or zapote blanco, is a native of the tropical highlands of Mexico and Central America. The custard apple is a common name given to the fruits of the Annona family. Many species have been cultivated in tropical countries around the world since the sixteenth century.

The white sapote has been growing in the United States since the 1800s. Growers are now increasing plantings anticipating greater demand as consumers become more familiar with its sweet, silky-smooth flesh.

The white sapote resembles an apple without the characteristic indentation at the blossom end. The fruit vary in size, but generally are 2 inches or more in diameter. Its skin is very thin, ranging in color from greenish-yellow to yellow.

The flesh of the white sapote has a tropical flavor uniquely its own, but with a bit of a combination of banana and papaya. Dotting its creamy flesh are usually one or more small oval-shaped pits and/or smaller, immature flattened seeds.

AVAILABILITY: Early fall through early winter.

SELECTION AND STORAGE: Choose firm fruit, free of bruises. Handle carefully because they bruise easily. Allow white sapotes to ripen at room temperature until they yield to gentle palm pressure, then refrigerate. They will keep a few days, but should be used promptly.

PREPARATION: The flesh can be spooned from the skin and used much like a ripe persimmon. For other uses, peel the fruit and cut the flesh from the pits. The thin, immature seeds are sometimes indistinguishable, so be sure to remove these entirely.

SERVING SUGGESTIONS:

- Chill and halve the sapotes, then squeeze the flesh with fresh lemon or lime juice and a sprinkling of sugar.
- Purée for a fruit sauce.
- Add sapote chunks or balls to fruit or poultry salads.
- Purée into fruit shakes, sorbets, or mousses.
- Drizzle chunks with orange or apricot liqueur.

NUTRITION INFORMATION: There are many types of sapotes and their nutritional value varies. White sapotes are a good source of vitamin C, provide potassium, and have about 125 calories in a $3^1/_2$-ounce portion.

SAPOTE-LIME PIE

Graham Cracker
Crust (see page 242)
1 1/2 pounds sapotes
2 or 3 limes
3/4 cup sugar, divided
1 envelope unflavored
gelatin

3 eggs, separated
1/2 cup milk
Sweetened whipped
cream
Lime slices for garnish

Prepare the Graham Cracker Crust and press into a 9-inch pie plate. Bake for 8 minutes. Cool.

Peel and pit the sapotes. In a food processor or blender, purée the sapotes and measure 3/4 cup purée. Grate enough lime peel to equal 1 1/2 teaspoons. Extract juice from the limes and measure 1/4 cup. Add the lime juice to the sapote purée.

In the top of a double boiler, combine 1/2 cup sugar and the gelatin. In a small bowl, beat the egg yolks and gradually add the milk. Pour the mixture into the top of the double boiler. Cook the mixture over boiling water for 4–5 minutes. Remove from heat. Stir the lime peel and the sapote purée into the gelatin mixture. Cover and chill for about 1 hour.

In a medium bowl, beat the egg whites until frothy. Gradually add the remaining 1/4 cup sugar, beating until stiff peaks form. Fold the egg whites into the sapote mixture. Spoon the sapote filling into the Graham Cracker Crust. Chill until firm. Serve with a dollop of whipped cream and garnish with twisted lime slices.

MAKES ONE 9-INCH PIE

SAPOTE VELVET

$3/4$ pound sapotes
$1/2$ cup light cream
$1/2$ cup milk

$1/4$ cup light rum
2 tablespoons honey
Crushed ice

Peel the sapotes, remove the seeds, and place fruit in a blender or food processor. Add the remaining ingredients and blend until smooth. Pour into glasses.

MAKES 4 ONE-CUP SERVINGS

HOT GINGER TURKEY AND SAPOTE ON SALAD GREENS

Marinated turkey is sautéed and served on a cool, crisp bed of salad greens.

Ginger Marinade (see page 109)
2 pounds uncooked turkey tenderloin
$1/3$ cup fresh orange juice, divided
2 tablespoons olive oil
$1/4$ teaspoon salt
Freshly ground black pepper

1 bunch watercress
2 cups torn romaine or Boston lettuce
1 cup coarsely shredded red cabbage
3 white sapotes
3 tablespoons peanut or vegetable oil

Prepare Ginger Marinade and pour into an 8-inch-square dish. Cut turkey into 2-inch strips about $1/2$-inch wide and toss strips in the marinade; cover and refrigerate at least 1 hour.

In a small bowl, combine 3 tablespoons orange juice, olive oil, salt, and black pepper to taste; mixing well. Rinse watercress, discarding thick stems, and place in a large mixing bowl. Add the lettuce and cabbage. Peel, seed, and slice the sapotes, moistening with the remaining orange juice; set aside.

Heat the peanut or vegetable oil in a wok or large skillet. Using a slotted spoon, lift about half of the turkey from the marinade and place in the skillet. Cook over medium-high heat about 2–3 minutes, or until golden brown and cooked throughout. Remove turkey from wok or skillet and set aside. Repeat with remaining turkey, adding a little more oil if needed.

Pour olive oil mixture over the salad greens; toss to coat. Divide salad greens among 4 dinner plates, arranging turkey in the center. Arrange sapotes over the greens and serve immediately.

MAKES 4 SERVINGS

$\mathcal{B}$IBLIOGRAPHY

Andrews, Jean. *Peppers: The Domesticated Capsicums.* Austin: University of Texas Press, 1984.

"Asian Pears" brochure, Phillips Farms & Universal Produce Corporation, Visalia, CA.

Bastyra, Judy and Julia Canning. *A Gourmet's Guide to Fruit.* Los Angeles: HP Books, 1989.

Beck, Bruce. *Produce—A Fruit and Vegetable Lovers' Guide Book.* New York: Friendly Press, 1984.

Brennan, Georgeanne and Charlotte Glenn. *Peppers—Hot and Chile*, Aris Books, Addison-Wesley, 1988.

Brown, Marlene. *International Produce Cookbook & Guide.* New York: Price, Stern, Sloan, 1989.

"California Artichokes," California Artichoke Advisory Board, Castroville, CA.

Composition of Foods: Fruits and Fruit Juices, USDA Handbook No. 8–9, Washington, D.C.: Human Nutrition Information Service, 1982.

Composition of Foods: Vegetables and Vegetable Products, Raw, Processed and Prepared, USDA Handbook No. 8–11, Washington, D.C.: Human Nutrition Information Service, 1984.

DeWitt, Dave and Nancy Gerlach, "The Whole Chile Pepper Catalog," Out West Publishing, 1987.

Food Composition Table for Use in Latin America. Institute of Nutrition of Central America and the National Institutes of Health, Bethesda, MD, 1961.

Ensminger, M. E., Audrey Ensminger, James E. Konlande, and John R. K. Robson, *Foods and Nutrition Encyclopedia.* Clovis, CA.: Pegus Press, 1983.

"Feijoas," *New Zealand Gourmet.* Auckland, New Zealand.

Grigson, Jane. *The Mushroom Feast.* New York: Knopf, 1975.

Grigson, Jane and Charlotte Knox. *Exotic Fruits & Vegetables.* New York: Henry Holt, 1986.

"Guide to Exotic Mushrooms," Frieda's Finest/Produce Specialties, Los Angeles, CA.

Hawkes, Alex D. *A World of Vegetable Cookery.* New York: Simon and Schuster, 1985.

"Hello Tamarillo," New Zealand Tamarillo Growers Association.

Hirasuna, Delphine. *Vegetables.* San Francisco: Chronicle Books, 1985.

Hom, Ken. *Asian Vegetarian Feast*. New York: William Morrow, 1988.

Leibenstein, Margaret. *The Edible Mushroom*. New York: Ballantine, 1986.

Morash, Marian. *The Victory Garden Cookbook*, New York: Knopf, 1982.

Nagy, Steven and Philip E. Shaw. *Tropical and Subtropical Fruits—Composition, Properties and Uses*. Westport, CT.: AVI Publishing, 1980.

The Packer's 1990 Produce Availability and Merchandising Guide. Overland Park, KS.: Vance Publishing, 1990.

Pijpers, Dick, Jac. G. Constant, and Kees Jansen. *The Complete Book of Fruit*. New York: Gallery Books, 1986.

"Quality Tropical Fruits and Vegetables" manual, Homestead, FL.: J. R. Brooks & Son, 1988.

Schneider, Elizabeth. *Uncommon Fruits & Vegetables—A Commonsense Guide*. New York: Harper & Row, 1986.

Spear, Ruth. *The Classic Vegetable Cookbook*. New York: Harper & Row, 1985.

"Specialty Fruits" and "Specialty Vegetables" consumer leaflets, United Fresh Fruit and Vegetable Association, Alexandria, VA.

"Sugar Snap Peas—A Sweet Surprise," *American Vegetable Grower*, Vol. 36, No. 5., May 1988.

Sunset Fresh Produce A to Z. Menlo Park, CA.: Lane Publishing, 1987.

"Supply Guide—Monthly Availability of Fresh Fruit and Vegetables," United Fresh Fruit and Vegetable Association, Alexandria, VA., 1989.

"Sweet Success: The Development of the Sugar Snap Pea," Rogers Seed Company, Boise, ID., 1988.

Tolley, Emelie and Chris Mead. *Cooking with Herbs*. New York: Clarkson N. Potter, 1989.

"White Sapote!," "Feijoa," and "Discover Cherimoyas" leaflets, California Tropics, Carpinteria, CA.